Biog

The Man Who Never Sleeps

The Man Who Never Sleeps

The Autobiography of Tom Bell OBE

338·092

With David Walker

The Book Guild Ltd

First published in Great Britain in 2019 by
The Book Guild Ltd
9 Priory Business Park
Wistow Road, Kibworth
Leicestershire, LE8 0RX
Freephone: 0800 999 2982
www.bookguild.co.uk
Email: info@bookguild.co.uk
Twitter: @bookguild

Typeset in Adobe Garamond Pro

Printed and bound in Great Britain by 4edge Limited

ISBN 978 1912881 000

British Library Cataloguing in Publication Data.
A catalogue record for this book is available from the British Library.

Printed on FSC accredited paper

Dedicated to the thousands of talented, innovative and hardworking staff of TNT UK & Ireland with whom I shared 33 years of my life, but most of all dedicated to Gina, my wife, in this our 40th year of marriage.

Tom Bell

Contents

Introduction

Tom Bell is the sort of bloke you'd want in your trench when the proverbial hits the fan. He's a fighter – he doesn't back down. More importantly, he's a winner. Never one to shirk a challenge, his 'can do' philosophy means he's always delivered the goods throughout his life. But don't take my word for it – ask Rupert Murdoch.

Murdoch – arguably the most powerful media mogul of modern times – needed help, as he sought to revolutionise Britain's national newspaper industry in the 1980s. Tom Bell was on hand to provide it. As Murdoch waged war on the left-wing print unions, he knew success hinged on whether he could get millions of copies of his News International titles past thousands of militant pickets.

During a bitter, bloody and violent industrial dispute lasting 54 weeks, Tom masterminded the breaching of the union battle lines that laid siege to 'Fortress Wapping'. Under his command, and working to his blueprint, TNT's fleet was the final piece of the jigsaw.

Murdoch would win, a 'New Sun' would rise and Tom's career star would be on an unstoppable upward trajectory.

Working up to 18 hours a day, Tom must've appeared indefatigable. Murdoch certainly thought so. He bestowed the title of this book, *The Man Who Never Sleeps* upon him. It was a much deserved compliment – recognition of a man who was destined for the top in a fast-moving, ultra-competitive, multi-billion pound global industry.

Having had next to nothing as a child, Tom knew that hard work, a sharp mind and an eye for business represented his only realistic hope of ever attaining the wealth and status he craved. Even from an early age he always had an idea of his worth. He knew what he could bring to the table. He knew he could add value. He just had to prove that a lad from a tenement in Kirkcaldy had what it took to succeed in life.

He was good with numbers. As he climbed the business ladder *(quite literally at one stage)*, he had the Midas touch. He pioneered new ventures and reversed the ailing fortunes of a pedestrian 'express' enterprise. Over a period of three decades he went from driving a lorry to driving up record-breaking year-on-year profits.

His insatiable appetite to make money was not only great news for his employers, it was a cash lifeline for a comparatively unknown children's charity. Tom was as ruthless towards his competitors as he was compassionate to those most in need. His ability to generate millions of pounds in donations provided a better quality of life for tens of thousands of mentally, physically and socially disadvantaged youngsters.

He set the bar, and he set it high. He presided over a corporate culture which placed quality and opportunity at the heart of the business. In his 20-odd years at the top of the management tree, he saw his various teams pick up 21 industry 'Oscars'. His career and charitable exploits didn't go unnoticed.

He's been honoured by the Queen, sat on a throne next to the Duke of Edinburgh, and was present in Buckingham Palace when a Royal tart went missing. He's been handcuffed to a World Heavyweight Boxing champion and hoodwinked by a robot from *Star Wars*.

He's wined, dined and fraternized with stars from the world of sport and music legends. He's been impressed by some and singularly unimpressed with others. Fair to say the wee lad born into a poor, working class Scottish family has done well for himself.

Having lived in England since he was nine years old, his accent totally belies his origins. The move south meant plenty of fights at school for the new 'Jock on the Block'. Tom was handy with his fists but eventually chose the path of least resistance, allowing his 'north o'er the border' burr to disappear. Nonetheless, he remains a fiercely patriotic Scot.

As a passionate football fan, he has a 'soft spot' for his first love, his hometown team, Raith Rovers. That fondness pales in comparison to the raging affair he's been having for the past six decades with Tottenham Hotspur. It continues to this day.

The contrast between little Raith of the Scottish First Division and the mighty Spurs of the English Premier League is a fitting analogy of Tom's life. He's gone from tough beginnings and living on homemade soup – *one where you were lucky if you found a piece of potato in the thin broth* – to dining out on the finest steaks in some of the world's best restaurants.

It's a story of rags to riches and one he'd like to share with you.

1

The writing on the wall

My bedroom 'wallpaper' was unusual to say the least – but it was all my mum and dad could afford. If I tell you it was pink and green and 'read' all over you'd probably be none the wiser, other than picturing something rather garish and very unconventional.

It wasn't as if I had any say in the decorating – I was a young lad with two loving parents who were doing their very best to raise me, despite living in nigh on poverty, on the east coast of Scotland in the early 1950s.

To my mum, Cathie and my dad, Charles, it made perfect sense to cover the walls of my tiny bedroom in The Pink and The Green of the Scottish national press. The colour combination might have hinted at psychedelic art, but nothing could be further from the truth.

The last thing I'd see each night, before the gaslight was extinguished in my often cold and damp surroundings, were the sports pages of the local rag emblazoned across the walls. The Pink carried the football results, The Green reported on the horse racing. So there I'd be, in my formative years, going to sleep every night surrounded by newspapers masquerading as interior decor.

Little could I have known that 30-odd years later I'd be playing my part in revolutionising the British newspaper industry, earning the nickname of 'The Man Who Never Sleeps' from the world's most powerful media mogul. How ironic.

I'd never previously thought about that paradox until it came to capturing my life story in this book. Had I done so, I might've shared it with Rupert Murdoch on one of those long and 'eventful' nights at Wapping in 1986.

I was 34 years old and masterminding the successful distribution of Murdoch's News International titles the length and breadth of Britain. It was the beginning of the end of Fleet Street, effectively breaking the stranglehold of the print unions on the newspaper industry and, with it, sparking the steady decline of trade union influence in the UK.

It's not something that would've been envisaged for a boy born into a poor, working class family on 14th February 1952, at the Forth Park Maternity Home, Kirkcaldy, in Fife.

My arrival into the world on Valentine's Day was surprisingly newsworthy. I was one of four generations of firstborn males in the Bell family, all alive and kicking at the same time. There was me, my dad, my grandad Tom and my great-grandad Charles. Prior to this there'd been my dad, grandad, great-grandad and great-great-grandad all breathing the same air. Going further back, the genetic tradition had begun with my grandad, great-grandad, great-great-grandad and great-great-great-grandad all being together in the 19th century.

The Fife Free Press loved the quirkiness of it all, duly running the story, accompanied by a formal portrait of the four of us.

Obviously I was none the wiser about the significance of the situation until I grew older. It didn't help that it wasn't featured in either The Pink or The Green, so there was no chance of me reading about it on my bedroom wall!

Mum and Dad may have been poor, but there was no doubting I was born into 'good stock' in our tenement home in Nichol Street, Kirkcaldy – a town referred to locally as Lang Toun.

The tenements were pretty grim, but it was a friendly neighbourhood with everybody in the same boat – we were all swimming against the tide. It helped to get along with the neighbours, especially when you had to share an outside toilet with them. Mum and Dad did just that with Pete and Fay from next door.

With the 'facility' located down a passageway, or put into local parlance, *'up the close'*, my home comprised two rooms. The largest was used as a living room, where all the cooking, eating and washing took place, while also doubling up as Mum and Dad's sleeping area.

The smaller room was my bedroom, one which I later shared with my younger brother Alan. He came along when I was two years old.

Alan was born at home. In those days it was usually only the first child who had the privilege of being delivered in the hospital. That had been me. I have vague recollections of my mum shouting out in pain, with Dad and Fay running around with pails of hot water and taking away pots of blood. It was all very confusing. Of course, there was the sound of a newborn baby's cry, but I didn't really understand what was going on.

With an extra mouth to feed, life was only going to get harder. Mum would look after us, while Dad grafted away 12 hours a day, doing hard physical labour at the local whisky distillery.

There weren't many – if any – perks with the job, but working in a distillery must have meant the occasional fringe benefit for Dad. On one such occasion I saw him getting off the local bus, pissed as a fart, with a teapot in his hand.

It'd been full of whisky. Judging by the state of him he'd drunk the lot. Unsteady, he weaved his way from the bus stop – quite an amusing sight, and not one I'd seen before – as he headed home to bed to sleep off his alcoholic over-indulgence. Yes, he'd soon be in the land of nod, but not before my mum had given him a right bollocking.

He didn't get drunk very often – he couldn't afford to – times were hard. He joined the Territorial Army to bring in some extra money. His 'military service' was accompanied by a cosy feeling for me and my brother as the perishing winter nights closed in.

As well as the desperately needed cash, Dad was given a standard issue army greatcoat. It immediately became an improvised duvet and, by God, what a difference it made. It was as if a magical heater had suddenly been switched on. For the next two or three winters we'd be as happy as pigs in muck, snuggled up under the heavy woollen fabric of Her Majesty's Army Reserve. It was one thing having the windows ice up on the outside, quite another to have them frosted over on the inside. Keeping warm was a real challenge. We couldn't afford proper coal. We had to get by on sea coal. We'd go out on the Town Beach and the adjacent Pathhead Sands at weekends, searching for our 'black gold'.

It cost nothing but our time. At low tide the beaches would be littered with the stuff, washed up from the various pits that lined the Firth of Forth. It'd take hours for the whole family to pick up a hundredweight – enough to keep us going for a week or so, depending on the plummeting temperatures.

Spurned by the Forth waters, the sea coal was like no other type of coal. It was sparkling clean and shone jet black. The fist-sized chunks resembled large black diamonds. The natural mineral beauty belied its status, as a second rate substitute for the premium charcoal. It would ignite by heating with the very minimum amount of kindling, before breaking up and 'spitting', emitting a whistling or hissing sound as it burned. These were welcome sounds; it meant we were warm. It meant my mum could cook something hot for our bellies.

We didn't lack for warmth in other ways. Mum would be affectionate when taking care of me and Alan. She compensated for the lack of love openly displayed by my dad. He loved us right enough, but we hardly saw him. He was busy trying to bring in the money and provide for us. At the age of just 16, Mum had lost her father – the grandad I never knew – to tuberculosis. I don't know whether that tragedy influenced her when she later became a parent herself, but she was a good mum and the driving force in our family. She was a large lady in the physical sense, with a big heart to match.

Dad was by far the quieter of the two. I don't really remember him saying too much when I was a little kid. He had a demanding and tiring job. Maybe he was just knackered at the end of the day and didn't fancy chatting. My grandad Tom was far more talkative and engaging with me. I'd spend a lot of time with him and my gran at their home – another tenement – at 20, West March Street.

He was very well known and respected in the town. Whenever I went to the Co-op, the fish and chip shop, the ice cream parlour or wherever, people would say, 'You're Tam Bell's grandson.'

He was very outgoing, funny, kind and hardworking. He once told me, 'It costs nothing to say hello.' It was an obvious truth. It was a sentiment which helped shape my personality at an early age and influence the man I would become. He was a coalman for the Co-op, making deliveries with his horse and cart – the horse was called Billy. I can recall Grandad coming in off his coal round, blackened face, filthy from the day's work, obviously drunk and carrying an empty money bag.

He didn't bother to wash. He just crawled into bed in the front room and was out like a light. He'd used the day's takings and got as drunk as a skunk. He hadn't stolen the money, he'd taken an impromptu loan from his employers. The Co-op didn't sack him, they just deducted it from his wages and life went on. Fair to say, Grandad was a real character, much loved and revered by me, the rest of the family and just about everyone who knew him.

How he got together with my gran I'll never know. Grandad was a proper drinker, whereas Gran never touched a drop of alcohol. Very strait-laced, she was a prim lady who'd spend the week wearing a protective pinafore, doing her chores, but always finding time to spend with me and keep me entertained. We'd play cards for hours on end, read the newspaper and listen to the radio in the evening. Come Sunday, Gran would always put on her best clothes and attend church – The Kirk, as it was better known. Religion was very important to Gran.

Wednesday was the highlight of the week for me, as it was the day the Corona Lemonade man made his delivery. Gran would store the bottles in the back room of the tenement – it was colder than any fridge. We never needed ice to cool the drinks.

My special treat was a glass of cream soda with a spoonful of ice cream – my gran's piece de resistance. When you hardly have a penny with which to scratch your arse, a Corona cream soda was one of life's luxuries.

Whereas we were undoubtedly impoverished, there were others in Lang Toun who'd be coining in a small fortune. Kirkcaldy's one and only real claim to fame was that as the world's leading producer of linoleum. For over 100 years it was the main product of the town and by far the biggest employer. There was an all pervading odour that used to dominate the senses. People would ask, 'What's that fucking smell?' The answer was the whiff of linseed oil which permeated the air. When my grandad had to finish his coal round with the Co-op, he ended up working at Barry's Linoleum Factory, as did my dad.

Like most places in Kirkcaldy we had lino on the floors. We could only afford to have it cut around the bed. It was too expensive to have it actually go under the bed. What was the point? We wouldn't be standing on it. It's a measure of how poverty stricken we were. We were living in the linoleum capital of the world but could barely afford the product.

By the time I was seven, the local council finally wised up. The tenements were condemned and demolished. We were on the move to a new home, complete with an indoor toilet – the Bell family's very own, exclusive, non-shared 'throne', and a bathroom.

The switch to a three-bedroom council house at 48, Athol Terrace meant 'hello' electricity and a 'goodbye' to gas mantles. Our new life on the sprawling Templehall estate was a real upgrade, but money was still tight. We lived on homemade soup. Lentils were the staple ingredient. If you found a piece of potato in your soup, you counted yourself lucky.

I remember finding a 10-bob note *(that's 50p nowadays, but it went a hell of a lot further in the 1950s)* on some wasteland between our house and the local shops. I came home and told my mum.

'Look what I found on the way to the shops.'

'What?'

'It's a 10-bob note,' I said, feeling rather proud of myself.

'Oh, that'd be the 10 bob I lost this morning,' replied mum, 'Well done, son,' she said as she took ownership of the pink-coloured banknote.

It must've been 20 years later that she confessed she hadn't lost the money. She'd lied. She explained that we were so strapped for cash she had to take the 10 bob off me. She'd felt guilty and ashamed for two decades, but there was never any reason in my eyes. She did what she had to do for her family.

What I do remember is that, shortly after giving her the 10-bob note, we all had a lovely fish supper instead of homemade soup. No coincidence there.

My mum had told me a white lie born out of necessity, but both she and my dad weren't above 'breaking the law'. It wasn't exactly grand larceny, but we never had a television licence. The move to Templehall meant we had electricity. We could have a TV, but we didn't have the money to buy the required licence. Worse still, we most certainly couldn't afford the fine if the dreaded TV Detector Van Man discovered our guilty secret. If disconnecting a TV aerial had been an Olympic event, Charlie Bell would have medalled each and every time. By God he was fast.

Living on the vast estate meant my extended family of aunts, uncles and cousins were now virtually on our doorstep. The Bells, the Barclays and the Stewarts were all within easy walking distance. They all rubbed along nicely. Family was important. I tended to gravitate more towards the Barclays – my dad's side of the family –

with his sister Nan, her husband Willie and my cousins, Ann, Rona and Aileen.

The three girls and I would spend endless hours together at Gran and Grandad's. It was a really warm, loving and easy going environment. Ann, Rona and Aileen would go round to Gran and Grandad's on a Saturday morning. They'd do some cleaning and help with the shopping. I enjoyed playing with them and being with them.

My relationship with their dad, my uncle Willie, was completely different. He was extremely left wing. I wasn't. Even though I was still at primary school I had very firm political views. It was weird and, I'll admit, I must've been unusual. We would have fierce debates which would rapidly boil over into arguments. Compared to Willie, Jeremy Corbyn would sound like Tony Blair. Fair to say he was left of left and then he'd take another left. We would rail against each other endlessly. We would agree to disagree on politics for decades, right up until the day he died. Willie was on the Executive of the Scottish Miners' Union. There was no actual religious service at his funeral – just speeches by the likes of Mick McGahey, the SMU leader and lifelong communist. I can't fully explain why I was so clued into politics from such a young age.

Coming from such a bleak, working class background, I must have stood out with my right-wing views. I just knew I wanted to achieve things in life. I wanted to better myself; I had ambition. I didn't want to want for anything.

When you consider my mindset from such an early age, it shouldn't have come as a surprise that I would later be instrumental in eroding the foundations of left-wing trade unions in Britain. As a youngster, I was within a school year of being a passing ship in the night with a future Labour Prime Minister, but my career, my destiny, lay on the road rather than any water.

2

From Scotland to Snodland

'Drink it all up, Tom, it's good for you,' said my teacher. As a six-year-old you tend to do as you're told at school, but this just wasn't right – it stunk to high heaven and tasted disgusting.

'It'll help build healthy bones,' implored the teacher. All I knew was I was about to puke up all over the classroom. Ordinarily, the small bottle of free school milk would have lived up to its billing as an excellent addition to my staple diet of homemade soup, but not when it'd been stuck up against a blazing hot radiator for half the morning.

I was violently sick and about to set out on 60 years of milk-induced trauma. To this day, milk has never again crossed my lips. I've tried drinking it, but the association with that wretched bottle of gunk has never escaped my memory.

It's often said that '*Your schooldays are the best days of your life*'. It's not a view to which I would wholeheartedly subscribe but, putting aside my curdled milk encounter, I did enjoy life at West School, Kirkcaldy. There was virtually nothing I didn't like doing.

My calculator was an abacus, my notebook was a piece of slate and some chalk. It was basic stuff. We were taught to read, write and become numerate – we didn't do maths, we did arithmetic.

We started each day reciting the alphabet and doing our 'times tables'. One year in, and I could do my 12x table with ease. Arithmetic was drilled into me day after day after day – I was good with numbers – it was to serve me well later on in life.

Unlike a boy in the year above me, I wasn't going to become Prime Minister, but I was going to do alright – more than alright. Gordon Brown, born one year and six days before me, would become the Right Honourable Member of Parliament for Kirkcaldy and Cowdenbeath, en route to occupying Number 10 Downing Street. He succeeded Tony Blair as Labour PM in 2007. Three years later he presided over Labour's failure at the General Election. He'd held onto his seat in the constituency of my birth, but not the reins of UK Government power. He stepped down from his job as Labour leader in 2010, the same year that I would call time on my working life. It's a tenuous link between the two of us, but there was nothing tenuous about our shared love for Raith Rovers, our local football team.

It was a love that intensified when, aged seven, I moved to Templehall and switched to Dunearn School. I was shown to my desk. I couldn't believe my luck. I would be sitting next to a lad called Willie McNaught Junior. His dad, Willie McNaught Senior, played at centre half for Rovers and Scotland. He would make 418 appearances for Raith before he finished playing – still a club record to this day.

Can you imagine the excitement of going round to your mate's house for a kick about and seeing one of the top footballers of the day? Of course, it was different back then; footballers weren't multi-millionaire icons who lived in their own 'bubble'. It was nonetheless a thrill.

Willie Jnr was a superb footballer. We played football every single day and night, along with Willie's little brother, Kenny. He was three years younger than us. We used to stick him in goal most of the time. 'Wee' Kenny went on to become a strapping 6ft centre back, winning the League Championship with Aston Villa in 1981 and the European Cup the following year. His career would also see him star for Everton, West Bromwich Albion, Manchester City and Sheffield United. He was a top-class defender. If truth be told, he wasn't bad in goal either!

Football was, and always has been, one of my passions. I'd go regularly to watch Rovers play at Stark's Park. Like all the little kids, I used to get in for free. I'd be swept up in the arms of either my dad or my grandad and lifted over the turnstiles. I vividly recall going to see Raith's first game under the club's new floodlights on 29th September, 1960. Ironically, it was against Aston Villa, Kenny's future employers. Considering the terraces were made from railway sleepers filled with cinders, having floodlights was a really big deal for Raith.

Grandad was a diehard Rovers fan. He seemed to know anybody and everybody in Kirkcaldy – I could never figure out how or why. Even so, it shouldn't have come as a surprise when he arranged for me to meet one of Scotland's greatest ever players, Jim Baxter.

'Slim Jim', as he was known, started his career at Raith before moving to Rangers where he became a household name. He later starred in a 3-2 win over England at Wembley in 1967 – a year after England had won the 1966 World Cup. Naturally, that win led every Scottish supporter to proclaim Scotland as World Champions – me included. It was a logical conclusion, wasn't it?

There was an English connection when it came to me becoming something of a football 'hero' among all my mates in Templehall.

It happened as a result of my dad going south in search of work. Barry's Linoleum Works was closing down. Job prospects were virtually nil in Scotland. Dad, our old neighbour Pete and my uncle Bert ended up finding new employment in Kent. Dad would send money home to ensure Mum, me, Alan and my baby sister, Sandra, were looked after as best he could. He was providing for us but we hardly ever saw him.

We were still living in straitened times so he could only afford to come home every six months or so. On one such trip he bought me a plastic football. To say I was chuffed was the understatement of the year. I was the only kid in the neighbourhood with a plastic football – talk about elevated status! I was already popular, with plenty of mates from school and playing football on the local green, but all of a sudden every lad in the locality wanted to be friends with me because I was the one with the Frido football.

Of course, I loved seeing my dad, but I'd adjusted to him not being around. I didn't miss him as much as I perhaps should have when he was working away. I was enjoying school, playing with my friends and spending lots of time with my cousins and Gran and Grandad. I had a busy and fulfilling life. That was all about to change.

I was nine years old when it was announced we were moving to England. I wasn't thrilled at the prospect. It was a foreign country. The people spoke a different language – well, that was my take on it. We were going to Snodland – a place I didn't believe even existed. I mean *'Snodland'* – what kind of a name was that? I'd heard about this mythical *'Snodland'* from Mum and Dad, but it was just a strange sounding place. It never seemed real. It was July 19th 1961. We travelled from Kirkcaldy to Kings Cross on a train service called the Aberdonian.

There was me, Mum, Alan, Sandra and my grandad setting out on this questionable adventure. I was told it was for the best, so I supposed a better life must lay ahead for us in *Snodland*. Mum wouldn't lie about something like that, would she? Dad met us at Kings Cross. So this was England. This was London.

Somehow half-a-dozen Bells squeezed into a black cab for the 25-minute taxi ride which took us to Charing Cross Station to catch the train to *'Snodland'*. It'd be another hour or so, and 36 miles, before reality really kicked in. We had to change trains at Strood, and the station tannoy whirred into action, 'The next train leaving platform four will call at Cuxton, Halling, Snodland, New Hythe, Aylesford, Maidstone Barracks and Maidstone West.' There was no turning back. There was a *'Snodland'* and we'd be there in three stops.

Snodland is situated on the River Medway, between Rochester and Maidstone. Postal pioneer Thomas Fletcher Waghorn – the man who shortened the 19th-century route to India from three months to 35 days by crossing the Egyptian desert – is buried in the local churchyard. 30 years after arriving in Snodland, I too would be something of a pioneer, only this time in the world of express parcels!

As we walked from the railway station to our new home, two things struck me. The first was a thatched house in the High Street – a Tudor Mulberry cottage – I'd never seen one before. It was totally different to Templehall's rows of anonymous council houses. The second was that all the doors of the houses were painted brown. Why brown? What a horrible colour. How unimaginative. As we turned into our new 'street' – Holborough Road – I saw all the doors on one side were still painted brown, but on the other side they were all painted blue.

I'd had 'The Pink' and 'The Green' in my bedroom as a kid, and yet here was a road limited to brown and blue. Maybe they'd had a job lot of paint and done it on the cheap? I couldn't get my head round it.

It turned out if you lived behind a blue door your dad worked for Blue Circle Cement in Snodland. If you lived behind a brown one, your dad worked for the Townsend Hook paper mill. The Bells would be behind a brown door at number 198. Even at a young age I found it bizarre that the colour of a door could dictate the destiny of so many people. They seemed resigned to working at a cement factory or a paper mill. This wasn't going to fit in with my aspirations. These houses didn't have drives. If they didn't have drives where was I going to park my fancy car?

After another 50 yards we reached our new home. I went inside. After a couple of minutes a horrible realisation dawned. We didn't have a proper bathroom. The toilet was 60 yards up the garden. We'd travelled 500 miles to a new life and effectively gone back in time, living in a tenement. I'd been told we were coming to England and life would be better. How was this better? At least we didn't have to share the outside bog with the neighbours. It was scant consolation.

I was back to having a weekly scrub up in a tin bath in front of the fire on a Sunday night. My sister would go first, my brother second and finally me. By the time it was my turn there'd be two loads of scum floating on the surface. I wasn't happy.

As if that wasn't bad enough, there'd be a musical accompaniment on the radio. The Mike Sammes Singers and 'Sing Something Simple' were synonymous with me sitting in tepid, murky water in our kitchen. God, how I hated that song as I sat in the muck of my siblings.

Years and years later I was staying at the St Brelades Bay Hotel in Jersey with my wife Gina. It was a birthday getaway break in what was an upmarket and very popular establishment. They'd iron your morning newspaper before bringing it to your room – how posh was that? The Channel Islands' favourable summertime climate was ideal for beautiful blooms. The hotel's floral arrangements and hanging baskets were very eye-catching. It was the sort of place that if a fuchsia head dared to drop from one of the hanging baskets, there'd be a member of staff on hand to catch it, before it hit the ground. You'd be in reception and hear people booking the same room for the same time the following year, as they checked out.

I went down to the bar one night and ordered a pint. The barman informed me they didn't serve pints. 'You'd better make it two halves then,' I said.

The barman said, 'What's the room number, sir?' I gave him the number.

'Oh,' the barman said in a surprised tone, 'I've not long had a request for a bottle of champagne to be sent to that room.'

'Yes, I know – I've drunk it! Now, could I have my two halves please?'

It was a nice place – a bit pretentious – but nice all the same. We were just about to step out onto the dance floor one night, when the

DJ announced, 'And next up is an all-time favourite of mine – 'Sing Something Simple' by the Mike Sammes Singers.'

'Sod this,' I said to Gina. 'Get yourself upstairs, get changed; we're off to the pub.' I just couldn't bear to listen to that bloody song and re-live bath time in Snodland. Most people have a 'soundtrack' of their lives, where certain songs evoke memories, both good and bad. I'm no different. There was no way I was singing something sodding simple!

Moving away from Scotland, from Gran and Grandad, Ann, Rona, Aileen and all my friends, was a bit of a wrench, but I was never homesick. Grandad had accompanied us on the journey to Kent, but he wasn't staying. Life in England didn't exactly get off to a flyer with the distinct lack of an indoor toilet, but I was just a kid. I'd soon adapt to my new environment and make new friends. We were back with my dad, united as a family and everything would be good.

It wasn't a time to dwell on what I'd left behind. My focus was on what lay ahead. I've always believed that in life you're dealt a certain hand – it's how you play it that counts. So, what did England have in store for a wee bairn from Kirkcaldy?

3

An English education

Violence and language difficulties were firmly on the curriculum as the autumn term began at St Katherine's Primary School, Snodland in September 1961. My classmates thought I spoke with a strange accent. I reckoned *they* were the ones who couldn't speak properly. The main difference was there were dozens of them and only one of me in our school year.

The Kent boys unwisely taunted the new boy from 'north o'er the border'. They soon found out actions spoke louder than words or, to be more precise, two fists from Fife spoke louder than any adolescent insults. I spent the first six weeks fighting my tormentors and making sure I was the last one standing. It wasn't how I wanted to start life at my new school, but I wasn't going to be bullied or have them taking the piss.

Despite taking on anyone who dared to ridicule my Scottish burr, I decided the path of least resistance would better serve me in the long run. It was easier to change my accent and blend in with my new surroundings than scrap with all comers. My Dad, bless him, who'd already been in Kent for a good two years before we moved down, never allowed his accent to be compromised by those around him. It wasn't such a big deal for the grown-ups, but kids are kids and they can be cruel at times.

My first school year in England was ridiculously easy. They were teaching the same stuff I'd already been taught in Scotland. I knew most, if not all, of the answers and appeared very clever. Don't get me wrong, I was a sharp lad, but my prior knowledge gave a false impression of my true academic acumen.

The teachers were soon very aware of 'the bright boy from Scotland'. 'You're going to go to university, Tom,' they told me. 'You're going to do this, you're going to do that.' In their eyes, the sky appeared to be the limit for me. It certainly appeared that way. Then along came the 11+ exam.

The all-important exam determined who'd go to the grammar school and who'd be consigned to the secondary school. I failed!

The headmistress couldn't believe it. My class teacher couldn't believe it. My mum certainly couldn't believe it. What the hell had gone wrong? I'd been on an upward trajectory since the beginning of term, but I was damned if I knew what had happened. Undeterred that her star pupil had faltered, the headmistress took me to Maidstone Technical School. The technical school specialised in a curriculum more tailored to producing tradesmen. Woodwork and metalwork took precedence over more academic studies. 'Don't worry, Tom, you'll be coming here in two years. You can take the exam again when you're 13. You'll be sure to pass.' Just why the headmistress thought I had a future as some sort of tradesman was beyond me. I was bloody useless with my hands, as my woodwork and metalwork teachers would readily testify. Amid huge disappointment, I was leaving primary education and off to the apparent ignominy of Snodland Secondary School. The first year went to plan. I was 'Top Boy' in the school – fifth overall, behind four girls. I was back on track. Mum was delighted.

Having me achieve 'Top Boy' status meant a lot to her. If truth be told, it meant quite a lot to me too. Dad was the odd one out. He wasn't unduly bothered one way or the other. I never figured out why. There were many facets to my father that I could never quite fathom. He was who he was and there was nothing I could do to change him. Unlike him I had dreams. I wanted a house with a drive, and a nice car sitting on that drive. I wanted to be a millionaire by the time I turned 40.

To say my second year didn't go as planned is like saying the Titanic came across a patch of ice. I plummeted from Top Boy down to 29th. It was my own fault. I'd spent it mucking around with my best mate Roland Day. Rather than buckle down and build on any academic foundations, I preferred to concentrate on earning a reputation as the biggest practical joker in the school. I lost all interest in the 13+ exam – the one that was supposed to guide me to technical school. I didn't even attempt it. For some reason best known to me, I decided I was happy at Snodland Secondary. I was at ease in that environment. I couldn't be arsed moving to another educational establishment. Whether I was stupid, short-sighted or just rebellious, it made no difference. My mum went apeshit and gave me the biggest roasting ever. She thought I was throwing away my best chance at a better life. On reflection, it was hard to argue with her logic, but at the time I thought I knew best.

I'd describe myself as confident, exuberant and mischievous. Contrary to what some of my teachers might have believed, I was never out of control. Even when I was playing up and being disruptive I knew exactly what I was doing. I made a conscious choice to 'live in the moment', enjoy life and have a bloody good laugh. My behaviour was detrimental to my studies. Watching my school grades drop off a cliff edge was a self-inflicted wound, but it wasn't the only price to pay for playing the fool.

Punishments of the day came in a variety of guises. You can forget your namby-pamby, liberal do-gooders of the modern day. They simply didn't exist in my schooldays. If you were naughty you got a clout. Corporal punishment was meted out on a regular basis. Parents simply accepted that if their 'little darling' had received a whack from a teacher, it must've been merited.

The staff at Snodland Secondary had a variety of weaponry to draw upon whenever I misbehaved. Dickie Spalls, the headmaster was a cane man. Mr Dods the woodwork teacher hit you with a dowel rod. Ken Coombes the sports teacher slapped you on the bare arse with his hand. Jimmy Boorman the metalwork teacher would hit us with a two-foot metal ruler – well, he did, until my mate Fred Huckson chopped it up into inch pieces on a guillotine!

The most infamous of the lot was my class teacher Don Lister. He'd hit you with a slipper, but not just any old slipper. Mr Lister operated his own penal code. It demonstrated a certain measured approach as judge and jury but, thankfully for me, not executioner. Even Snodland Secondary drew the line at capital punishment. Lister's Law meant the size of the slipper administered to your backside would be governed by the magnitude of the 'offence' you'd committed. Let me give you a case study involving yours truly.

I'd had a run-in with this other kid one morning. The bad blood between us was still boiling when the bell went for lunch break. School dinners at Snodland Secondary would see pupils carry two plates – one for the main course and one for pudding. We'd operate a rota where a pupil would be nominated to pour gravy onto one plate and custard on the other. I was on duty and 'accidentally on purpose' covered this other boy's thumbs in piping hot gravy and custard.

I executed my cunning plan with expert precision and timing, or so I thought. The lad yelped as the bubbling Bisto and custard washed over his thumbs, causing him to drop his plates. The cheers rang out around the canteen. It was always a source of amusement when crockery smashed. I remember thinking, 'mission accomplished'. Well, it was, until I heard Mr Lister. 'Bell, what do you think you're doing?'

Shit! Where had he come from? 'I don't know, sir. I slipped. It was an accident, sir,' I said, totally lacking in any conviction. Resistance was futile. I was banged to rights. No discussion, no argument, judgement had already been passed under Lister's Law.

'That's the slipper for you, lad – what size do you think it should be?'

'I don't know, sir.'

'Go to my room and bring back a size 10.' It was only one off the top of the scale. At least I'd swerved a size 12.

This was standard procedure. I had to go up to his room, rummage through an assortment of footwear on top of his cupboard, locate a size 10 plimsoll and take it back to him. It's the closest I ever came to experiencing how a turkey must feel in the approach to Christmas. I handed Mr Lister his weapon of choice and prepared for my punishment. What made it worse was Mr Lister always took a 10-foot run up before whacking you across the backside. Even that didn't act as a deterrent. Roland and I were always up to something. No two ways about it, we were little sods.

Our woodwork class backed onto the girls' home economics lessons. We'd wait for break time and nip into the class and nick a load of cakes, pastries or fruit salads – whatever the girls had made that lesson. We'd cart off as much as we could carry and sell them to the other kids in the playground. It was a brilliant scam with an immediate return on sales. How we ever thought we'd get away with it I don't know. Talk about naive. I narrowly escaped punishment when another food-related caper went wrong.

The school had extensive grounds, so much so that we could grow our own produce such as vegetables and soft fruits. We also had a small farm where we kept chickens, so there were always plenty of eggs. One day I decided I was going to take some home. I filled my pockets. It was only mid-morning. How on earth I thought I was going to get through the rest of the day without breaking any of them, I simply can't explain. Within 20 minutes I'd been caught with more than half a dozen eggs about my person. I claimed I was taking them to the canteen to give to one of the school cooks. Incredibly, the teacher believed me. He must have credited me with more sense than I had – I mean, who'd pinch eight or nine eggs and expect them to survive unbroken for the rest of the school day?

For saying I was supposed to bright, I didn't half pull some daft and ill-conceived stunts. We'd had an art exam one afternoon and Roland and I decided to sneak back into the art room after school had finished for the day. We laid all the paintings out and ruined each and every one by brushing water over them. We spared two of the 'exhibits' – mine and Roland's – obviously. That way we'd get the best marks in the exam, wouldn't we? It didn't take a genius to work out who was guilty. Once again, it wasn't one of my best plans.

Annie Beale, the art teacher, gave us four of her best with the slipper. It hurt like hell, but you couldn't show you were in pain. You'd lose face with your classmates if you did. On this occasion there was to be a sting in the tail. The next morning Mrs Beale came into school with her arm in a sling. She'd overdone it tanning our backsides and injured herself. It was a crazy kind of karma.

I'd do stupid things as a kid. I never thought through the ramifications but was always prepared to take the consequences. Corporal punishment had its place in my schooldays and, if truth be told, never did me any long-term harm. Perversely, it didn't stop me from being naughty. What it did do was set out parameters which I knew I mustn't go beyond. It helped maintain acceptable levels of discipline, sadly lacking in schools today. Corporal punishment should never have been banned. Liberal lefties won the day and nowadays teachers aren't allowed to lay a finger on any child. As a consequence we have rising levels of knife crime, assaults, bullying and God knows what else going on in Britain's schools.

I always paid my dues when I misbehaved, I accepted I was in the wrong, but there was one evil bastard who always had it in for me no matter what I did. Mr Cowell, the maths teacher, took exception to me simply because I had long hair and refused to conform when told to get it cut. He was a sadistic twat. He hated me. He didn't need a bona fide reason to be violent towards me. He just liked hitting me. He should never have been allowed to be a teacher.

One lunchtime he told me to stay back after the bell. He waited until the other kids had gone and the room was empty. He shut the classroom door and proceeded to beat the crap out of me. He slammed me against a radiator and kept belting me on the head with a blackboard rubber. He completely lost it, calling me all the names under the sun.

I was shit-scared. He was really laying into me as the blows rained down on my head, neck and the tops of my shoulders. The cunning bastard was careful not to mark my face. I didn't know when he'd stop or how far he'd go. I was frightened – genuinely frightened – but I sure as hell wasn't going to let the fucker see he'd hurt me. The attack must've only been for a minute or so – it seemed much longer. 'Let that be a lesson to you, Bell,' he said in a clinical, cynical tone as the beating ended and he regained his composure. I wanted to smash the bastard in the face.

I went to see Dickie Spalls the headmaster and put in a complaint. Cowell wasn't reprimanded. It was his word against mine. I didn't tell my mum and dad. In those days, if a teacher hit you, most parents would've sided with the teacher. The child must've done something wrong to merit the punishment. Even though I had the marks and bruises where he'd struck me, I couldn't prove it was him or that the attack had been unprovoked. There'd been no witnesses, Cowell had made sure of that. The only good thing to come of it was that I moved out of his maths lessons. Maybe Spalls suspected I was telling the truth but either couldn't, or wouldn't, go against Cowell. At least I wasn't doing algebra anymore. I hated bloody algebra. I was back doing arithmetic, which I much preferred. The only problem was I now had an Indian teacher and I couldn't understand a word he said.

Even though Cowell was no longer teaching me, I would fall foul of him one more time before leaving school. One of my proudest moments was being named Snodland Secondary School's Sports Captain. I'd only just earned the exalted status when I was promptly banned from representing the school at any level because of my luxuriant locks! How stupid was that? It was petty and childish and Cowell was behind it. I was backed into a corner. Either have my hair cut or sacrifice playing sports for the school.

I wouldn't give in, on principle. I kept my hair long and, consequently, my school sports career was extremely short. I retained the title of Captain and my status as a prefect, but it was a farce. I would never again represent the school in any sporting capacity. It was their loss.

My long hair did, however, help out in the pursuit of other, non-conventional 'sports' areas, namely girls. I was made to sit with the girls in most of my classes. It was seen as some sort of punishment. It had the opposite effect. I was at ease with the girls; they liked me and I liked them. I was never short of female company. My 'education' with the fairer sex advanced well – very well actually – in one of the school cloakrooms.

It was among the duffel coats, satchels and sports bags that I first encountered a girl's 'roll-on' – extremely tight-fitting underwear which held everything in and enhanced a girl's figure. One of the girls fancied me so we snuck off to the cloakroom for a snog and some fun.

After playing with her boobs, I went for the 'bulls-eye'. She was wearing a roll-on. After a couple of minutes of probing and fondling I reached my destination. By then I'd lost all the feeling in my fingers – the roll-on had cut off the blood supply to my hand. It wasn't quite the 'sensation' I'd had in mind.

I did, however, manage to be something of a sensation – along with Roland – in a most unexpected way. We were both extroverts and would play up to an 'audience', whether it was in class or out on the playground. We weren't shy and we liked being the centre of attention, albeit usually for the wrong reasons. It came as a shock when we landed the leading roles in the school drama – Tom Sawyer and Huckleberry Finn. This was different. This wasn't just being ourselves and messing about. This was being given responsibility, having someone put their faith and trust in us.

This was about not screwing up and letting everybody down. Neither of us had ever done anything like it, but Mr Bampton the drama teacher had every faith in the two of us. All the bravado, the fluff and bluster, which we'd be full of on a regular school day, went right out of the window. Mr Bampton – a teacher I remember with great fondness – had found a way of putting young Bell and Day on the back foot. We were so nervous as we stood behind the stage curtains on the opening night. We could hear the buzz of anticipation going round the school hall, packed with proud and expectant parents, grandparents, other family members and friends. We'd better not mess it up. The laugh would be on us if we got it wrong. It would be embarrassing. We wanted to do well for ourselves and we didn't want to disappoint Mr Bampton.

We were good. In fact, we were very good. We earned a standing ovation. We were chuffed with ourselves. It was to be my one and only public speaking 'engagement' for many years. That would later change with my rise through the senior managerial ranks at TNT. Over a period of time, addressing large audiences at business conferences or seminars became almost second nature. I'd always have Mr Bampton to thank for putting me on the right road. He was one of the good guys, doubling up as both a drama and French teacher. I both liked and respected him, but I couldn't stand French. When the School Leaving Certificates came around – the equivalent of today's GCSEs – the school insisted I took French. It was the only one of eight subjects taken that I failed. I passed seven, gaining two distinctions along the way – English Literature and Gardening – how diverse was that? A little bit like my acting debut, my gardening skills would also come in handy during my career with TNT.

All things considered, I enjoyed my time at Snodland Secondary. Although I hadn't gone to grammar school or the technical college, I'd emerged with a decent set of qualifications. It offered me a springboard to higher education opportunities.

It'd been a while since Don Lister had hit me with a size-10 slipper. I'd finally got my act together. Mr Lister said I should go to college. He was convinced I'd do well. At 15 years old I had the option of going to work full-time or burying my head in books. I'd been making money since I was 12 and already had a tidy little business going cleaning windows. It was time to make a decision.

4

Four-letter words

Work is a four-letter word, just like rich and poor. Even as a kid in Kent, I knew if I was to go from rags to riches, the only avenue open to me was hard work. I had a strong work ethic – I always have – and just like any other youngster I wanted 'nice things'. But they didn't come free; they had to be earned. The only way I'd get them was if I worked my balls off.

In the summer of 1967 I managed to get a job at the Townsend Hook paper mill during the school holidays. There was a certain inevitability that I'd wind up working at the mill – my dad worked there and I was living behind a brown door. It was the Snodland way of doing things. I swept floors, cleaning up waste paper – they called it 'broke' paper – paper that was flawed, imperfect, not fit for purpose. I was the 'Broke Boy', collecting all the sub-standard paper for recycling. Given my impoverished start in life, it seemed somehow appropriate.

It was a crap job, but I just got on with it, working conscientiously and trying to make a good impression. The new school term began, and for the first fortnight I went back to my studies. That changed when the paper mill phoned and asked if I'd like to work full-time in the Wages Office. It wasn't a difficult decision. All my mates had left and were earning. I told Mr Lister I was off and my schooldays were over. I started on £5 a week. I was now a 'working man', but a not very well paid 'working man'.

It was all about making 'dough', something I'd started doing three years earlier. I'd been delivering rolls for a local baker but was sacked after just a month. I was only 12 and was breaking the law. I couldn't be employed until I was 13. My 13th birthday dawned and the baker took me back on in an instant. Even though I'd previously lied about my age, I'd impressed him with my willingness to work. It was a 4am start, mixing the dough and baking the rolls, before delivering them to people's front doors. As if that wasn't enough, I had a morning paper round and an evening round. My life was bread rolls, newspapers, school and more newspapers.

Within a few months I was literally going up in the world, climbing the business ladder, as me and my mate Mick started cleaning windows.

We'd do the villages of Halling one week and Upper Halling the following week. We invested in sets of ladders, buckets and chamois leathers and just went for it. We'd knock on doors, canvassing for customers.

'Good morning. Would it be alright if we clean your windows for free?' That part of the sales pitch went down a storm. The second part would clinch the deal, 'And, if you're happy with them, will you pay us to clean them every fortnight?' The answer was invariably 'Yes'. We'd work all day Saturday and Sunday mornings. We did a good job, the customers could clearly see it, and we were each earning £7 a week. I'd work while others would play. When most of the country was glued to the TV watching England and West Germany in the 1966 World Cup Final, I was up a ladder doing the windows of the Plough Public House in Halling. I caught a glimpse of the first half through the pub windows. As a fiercely patriotic Scot, it wasn't that much of a sacrifice missing England being crowned World Champions. Nonetheless, my passion for football remained, but watching Raith Rovers was well and truly a thing of the past.

Pragmatically, I switched my allegiance to the club nearest to Snodland – Gillingham FC. I persuaded my mum that I'd be alright and keep out of harm's way on my frequent trips to the Priestfield Stadium. Half a crown would buy me a day out. It covered my train fare, a bag of chips before the game, entry to the ground, a match day programme and, finally, a box of Paynes Poppets – chocolate-covered toffees – for the journey home. As luck would have it I was supporting The Gills when they won their first ever championship. I was 12 years old when, with Freddie Cox as manager, they topped the old Fourth Division in what was – and still is – the tightest league title finish in Football League history. With Gillingham locked at the top with Carlisle United, on 60 points each, the champions and runners-up places were determined by goal average, distinctly different to the goal difference criteria applied nowadays. Gillingham's 1.967 goal average per game just edged Carlisle's 1.948. I was quite happy watching Gillingham on a regular basis, until Billy Thompson – a neighbour who was a couple of years older – persuaded Mum that I was old enough to go up to London to watch First Division football. He would take me to see his team, Tottenham Hotspur.

We'd go to maybe five or six games per season, catching an early train to London Bridge, before carrying on into central London. Billy would make the most of each trip, taking me to see tourist attractions such as The Monument, St Paul's Cathedral, Trafalgar Square, The Tower of London, Big Ben and Buckingham Palace, prior to the games. As a kid, I never dreamt I'd ever go inside 'Buck House', let alone meet the Queen. I enjoyed the historical aspects of each visit to the capital, but the main event was always to be found at White Hart Lane. We'd take the train to Bruce Grove Station, walk down the High Road and be there for when the turnstiles opened at 1pm. First in meant we could get a good vantage point at the front of the stand. I used to take a four-legged stool to ensure I'd be able to see the game.

I wasn't much good in woodwork class, but I did manage to make this stool. It'd taken me several terms to produce – the rest of the lads had long moved on to other wooden creations – but it literally stood me in good stead. I never missed any of the action. Yes, it was a bloody nuisance carrying it around London all day, but I managed. I'd have the stool in one hand and a wooden rattle in the other. I had my hands full alright.

My first game was against Sheffield United in the opening fixture of the season. Saturday August 22nd 1964 was the start of a love affair which continues to this day. Spurs won 2-0. The atmosphere created by a 60,000+ crowd was amazing. The day was unforgettable. I was so thrilled to be there, watching the likes of Danny Blanchflower, Dave Mackay, Bill Brown, Cliff Jones and Jimmy Greaves. I was hooked. From that day on, Spurs were the team for me. Not only would I be a fan for the rest of my days, I'd also strike commercial deals with the club for the benefit of TNT and our customers.

I'm eternally grateful to Billy for taking me to Spurs. Each trip was a well-earned reward to myself. I was showing initiative and grafting, but there were only so many hours in a day. I couldn't juggle my time to cover all my jobs and, at that time, my schoolwork. I ditched the bread rolls run and subbed out the evening paper round to my brother. I insisted on taking a commission off Alan. My business acumen was already coming through.

Nonetheless, I was spending just about everything I was making. Apart from Spurs, I loved music and fashion. The money would go on records and clothes. I was a Mod, so it was winklepicker boots and mohair suits for me. Even in those days, a decent mohair suit could knock you back £50. Looking good didn't come cheap. Mick, my friend and business partner, was a year older than me.

He was saving for a scooter for his 16th birthday. Eventually he had enough to buy a brand spanking new, shiny Vespa – every Mod's preferred mode of transport.

The first day he had it, he came down the road, let the clutch out, lost control, went flying across a junction and straight into a wall. He escaped with a few bumps and bruises. The Vespa wasn't so fortunate. It was left mangled and dented. Mick's ego was similarly bent out of shape.

With a full-time job at Townsend Hook to occupy me, Mick and I decided to sell the window cleaning round. A company – New Century Cleaning – bought it for £300 and we split the money 50:50. My £150 share of the proceeds was the equivalent of 30 weeks' pay in the Townsend Hook Wages Office.

I'd ditched my education for full time work, but I hadn't done it to pick up a pittance. I wanted more. Within five months I was promoted into the production department and, soon after, into the purchasing department. As Assistant Purchasing Manager, I worked for Mrs Mayo – a truly fearsome woman. She was a right old battleaxe, smoked like a trooper and didn't take any prisoners. For some reason, she took a shine to me.

I worked hard, was reliable and always on time. She was good at her job, very disciplined and meticulous in her record keeping. She wasn't everybody's cup of tea, but I picked up some good work habits from Mrs Mayo.

At 21 years old I was on £18 a week. Some of my mates were earning double. I needed a pay rise. If you don't ask you don't get, so I asked Townsend Hook for a very specific pay increase. I wasn't being greedy. I'd done my research and compared what I was getting with other mill workers. I wanted £28 a week. It wasn't a negotiating stance. I was easily worth £28. They offered £20. I told them to stuff it. I walked out there and then.

Later that same day I started at Reed Packaging. I was swapping office work for the shop floor. I'd be packing boxes. Not the most glamorous of roles, but the pay was better. The ease with which you could get a job in the 1960s was incredible.

It wouldn't happen nowadays. Technological advances and automated processes have wiped out the requirement for millions upon millions of jobs. It was so different 40 or 50 years ago. You could change jobs at the drop of a hat – walk out of one job and get another straight away. Employment was bountiful.

I was enjoying life as a bit of a 'lad', playing the field and generally having a good time with the local Maidstone girls. The older blokes on the shop floor would be living vicariously through my exploits. They'd ask, 'What did you get up to last night?' They'd want all the sordid details. What did she look like? Did she have big tits? Was she a blonde or a brunette? I told this one bloke that I'd met a girl at The Westerner – a local nightclub – and gone back to her parents' house on East Malling's Clare Park estate. We'd had some fun and done the 'business' while her mum and dad were asleep upstairs, blissfully ignorant of what was happening on their settee.

It turned out it was his daughter and I'd been in his house. He went absolutely ballistic! He wanted to punch my lights out. How dare I talk about his daughter like that? How dare I have sex with her? It was all very well him getting the rundown on who I was shagging, but not if it was his daughter. I could understand him being pissed off, but it was the height of hypocrisy. We had to be separated and work at opposite ends of the factory. It was the only way to keep the peace. I was quite glad of the 'excitement'. The job was mundane, to say the least, and the shift patterns were a nightmare. I found out if I volunteered for overtime I could get a regular 6am-6pm one week and 6pm-6am the following week.

They were long shifts, but at least you could plan a social life outside of work. The longer hours meant more money. It was a vital factor. I needed as much money as possible. I was going on my first ever foreign holiday. I was going to Malta on an adventure with two of my best mates, Ken and Frank.

On FA Cup Final day – May 5th 1973 – Don Revie's mighty Leeds United were playing Sunderland, the rank outsiders from the Second Division. The underdogs from the North East would cause one of the biggest FA Cup upsets of all time and win 1-0 in the pouring rain at Wembley. I couldn't give a monkey's. I was at

Gatwick Airport heading to the sunshine and a whole summer in Malta.

I'd only ever flown once before; it was a little plane down to Jersey. It hardly qualified me as a jetsetter. My only taste of 'international travel' had come 11 years earlier on the Aberdonian train down to King's Cross. I'd classified England as a foreign country when we moved to Snodland. I was as excited as I'd ever been about anything in my life. I'd been doing 12-hour shifts at Reed Packaging for months on end, saving every penny I could. I had a holiday budget and a plan.

I was heading for the heat of the Mediterranean and staying for as long as I could – until the money ran out. It wasn't much of a strategy but it'd do for me. We'd chosen Malta because Ken had a Maltese background and relatives living on the archipelago. There wouldn't be any language barriers and Ken knew his way around. Our mate Frank was married, but he was adamant he was coming with us. We couldn't see how he was going to manage it. His wife, Gaynor, was a girl I used to sit next to at St Katherine's Primary School. Why would she agree to her husband disappearing off to Malta for a few months with two confirmed bachelors?

Frank kept dropping off items of clothing at Ken's house in the weeks running up to our departure date. He was slowly assembling his holiday 'wardrobe' without Gaynor noticing. 'I'll be there, lads, don't you worry; just leave the wife to me – no problem!' We had to admire his optimism, or maybe he was just bullshitting.

Fair play to Frank. He rolled up at Gatwick. 'See, I told you I wouldn't let you down.'

'Yes, I know, but how the hell did you get Gaynor to let you come?' I asked. 'We'll be gone for a couple of months; she must be very understanding.'

'Oh, no worries. I just told her I was popping out to get a Chinese takeaway,' replied Frank. We couldn't tell if he was serious or joking. The main thing was we were getting on a plane bound for Luqa Airport, south west of the capital, Valetta.

When we did finally return in the September, Frank had the front to tell Gaynor that, 'There'd been one helluva queue at the Chinese.' Needless to say, the marriage didn't survive.

There's something very special about your first time abroad – going into the unknown – especially back in1973. We didn't even have the likes of Judith Chalmers and *Wish You Were Here* to give us a heads-up. ITV's holiday programme didn't make it to the screen until January 1974. Of course, Ken had told us a bit about the place. It was one thing trying to picture it, but quite another actually being there. Malta was superb. It was everything I dreamed it would be.

We were renting a flat in Pieta. It was to be our base until the money ran out. Then, and only then, would we be heading back to England and reality. As it turned out, our money lasted a lot longer than it should have done, thanks to the head barman at the Pieta Hotel – a local called Charlie.

We'd been in Malta for a week and met Charlie on the beach in Mellieha Bay. He told us where he worked and suggested we went down for a few drinks. The hotel was full of German tourists who would unwittingly keep me, Ken and Frank in food and beer for days on end.

The Maltese hated the Germans for the horrors the Nazis had inflicted upon them. Between June 1940 and November 1942, Hermann Göring's Luftwaffe had mercilessly bombed the island throughout a siege that lasted two years, five months, one week and two days. Malta had been of great strategic value in helping achieve Allied success in North Africa, but at a great cost. Hitler's Air Force and Mussolini's Regia Aeronautica (Italian Royal Air Force) flew more than 3,000 bombing raids over the country.

The German holidaymakers of 1973 paid a heavy price for the wartime aerial bombardment, namely keeping three boozy Brits in free beer and grub night after night after night.

Every time the Germans ordered a round of drinks, Charlie would give us a Hopleaf beer or a Cisk lager and put it on the

Germans' bill. Every time the Germans ordered food, we had a free bite to eat. Charlie played a blinder. I don't know who enjoyed it more, Charlie or us, but it saved us a small fortune. Knowing the arrogant, unsuspecting Germans were spending their Deutsche Mark travellers cheques on us made the chilled beers even more refreshing. Just imagine how many extra sunbeds the Germans could have had, if they'd not spent so much on us.

German generosity was a big help when we wanted to hire a car. We had more money than we'd anticipated. We asked Charlie where we could hire a cheap car. He said his brother had a garage in Hamrun. He'd be able to fix us up. He did us a cracking deal on a red Triumph Herald Convertible. It was a terrific little runner, apart from the gearbox being a bit cranky.

There wasn't much of Malta that that car didn't cover. After a month of happy motoring and with money running low, we were resigned to taking it back. Amazingly, the best value for money hire in the history of car rentals was about to get even better.

Charlie's brother – for the life of me, I can't remember his name – gave us the deal of all deals, one which typified the easy-going Maltese lifestyle.

'You can't afford to keep it? Don't worry, you keep it until you're ready to go back home, but then you do me a big favour in England.'

'Sounds pretty good to me,' I said. 'What's the favour?'

'You get me some grommets for the gearbox and we'll call it all square.'

Were we hearing him right? 'Sorry, say that again,' said Ken.

'The gearbox – it's not the best. I need grommets to fix it. You can keep the car for as long as you're here, but you must promise to send me grommets from England.' We couldn't believe it. We had that car for another two months, all for the price of eight packets of grommets. One of the first things we did when we returned home was pop down to Parkfoot Garage on Maidstone's London Road. Each packet of grommets cost half a crown. We just went crazy and blew a whole £1, plus postage and packaging, and sent eight packets out to Malta. We heard back that Charlie's brother was ecstatic when his parcel arrived.

Malta was everything I hoped it would be, and more. We soaked up the sun, had loads of fun, explored the island and absorbed the history and culture. I loved it. We went back the following summer, and I've holidayed there many times.

I've a real affinity for the place. In 1978 it would play its part in confirming that the love of my life was destined to be my wife.

5

A knight of the road

For a man determined to succeed in life I was lacking a sense of direction. Nobody could, or would, ever doubt my capacity to put in a shift, but I wasn't going anywhere fast in my early 20s. I had no career path, I was taking jobs either side of holidays in Malta with Frank and Ken. I worked as a dumper truck driver for Tilbury Construction and later as a fitter's mate at Rugby Cement in Halling. It wasn't very inspiring.

By this time Frank was a heavy goods vehicle (HGV) driver on really good money. If he could do it I could do it. I needed a HGV Class 1 licence to be able to drive the 32-ton wagons. There was one problem: I couldn't afford the two-week driving course. I could barely stretch to the cost of a week's training, but I had to find a way to get that licence. The course was designed to take a HGV Class 2 driver up to HGV Class 1 standard.

I rang the instructor running the training and asked, 'Could I just skip the HGV 2 training and go straight to HGV 1?'

'It's unorthodox and not many can do it, but if you want to try I'm happy to give it a go,' was his response.

I spent 35 hours over a five-day period manoeuvring this 30-foot-long wagon all over the shop. It was a steep learning curve but I had a natural aptitude for it. The training went well. I was confident and the instructor had every confidence in me. The test followed on immediately after the training. I took it. I failed. Bollocks!

I'd only just missed it by a small margin, but a re-test could take weeks, even months, to come through. I was lucky. There was a cancellation the following week. I grabbed the slot, took the test and nailed it. I was fully qualified – a knight of the road – set fair to conquer the highways of Britain, or so I thought. There was a degree of romanticism about 'life on the open road'. The reality was very different.

I went looking for a job, only for each application to be met with the same negative response, 'You've no experience; we only want experienced drivers.' Talk about chicken and egg – how the hell could I gain experience if nobody would give me a chance? Eventually I had to make do with a job at a tipper company. It wasn't what I wanted, not what I'd envisaged when I passed the HGV 1 test. I hated it, but I stuck at it until the night they fired me.

I was making a delivery to site when a mechanical malfunction caused the truck to tip too soon – 12 tons of tarmac slid off the back, ending up heaped on the floor. The site foreman was very understanding. He could see it hadn't been my fault and he signed for a 'cold load' – tarmac which had been delivered but couldn't be used. It meant my employers wouldn't lose out – they'd still get paid. I didn't get back to the yard in Bearsted until eight o'clock in the evening. I'd been gone so long the company were considering sending out a search party. I told them what had happened. They listened, and then the bastards sacked me.

At least I now had some experience, even if it hadn't been the best. It helped me get a job with J&L Smith – a bit of a cowboy outfit – run by two brothers, John and Len Smith. I was determined to hold this job down; I couldn't afford another screw-up.

On day one they sent me to Reeds paper mill in Aylesford and then on a run up to Camberley in Surrey. I was expected to 'sheet and rope' a wagon for the first time in my life – basically covering the load in a protective tarpaulin sheet and securing it with ropes tied with 'dolly knots', so called because they resembled peg dolls.

The run to Camberley was fine, the paper duly delivered. The return trip meant collecting a consignment from Johnson's Chemicals and then back to Maidstone. I applied my new-found skills and set off. Within minutes I couldn't see a bloody thing out of my mirrors. The sheeting was blowing everywhere. Half a mile down the road, the cops pulled me over.

Not only was it not secured properly, the words 'THIS SHEETING HAS BEEN STOLEN' was printed in capital letters, the whole length of the trailer. I explained it was my first day and I didn't really know what I was doing. The officers had a laugh at my expense and told me to be on my way. It was a lesson learned. Within a week I was an expert at sheeting and roping, as if I'd been doing it all of my life.

I'd spend the next couple of years trudging up and down the country, setting off at shit o'clock, driving all day and sleeping in the cab at night. It wasn't glamorous, but I'd get 20% of whatever the lorry earned each week, plus the statutory 'night out' money. I was on £200 a week and moving in the right direction.

Coming from Kent meant I'd always be on long runs. The M25 didn't exist so it'd be the Blackwall Tunnel, up through Hackney to the North Circular at Wembley and then onto the M1, stopping at Toddington Services for breakfast. If I was going up the A5, I'd stop at the Canary Cafe, which is now the Jurys Inn Hotel at Hinckley Island.

An overnight run would often mean a sleepover at The Red Lion on the A45 at Northampton. It was in a central location and very popular. The publican had installed proper showers and toilets – specifically for the drivers. It was a mini utopia. Personal hygiene could be a real challenge on some of the overnight runs and the landlord had obviously done his homework. He knew what his customers wanted, and he'd have dozens of sweet smelling, beer drinking drivers all week long! They'd be downing pints late into the night and, more often than not, getting on the road at 4am and 5am. Looking back, it wasn't clever – God knows how many would've failed breathalyser tests – but it was just the way of the world in the 70s.

It was the same with driving hours. Tachographs weren't around and there's many a time I'd drive 'illegal' – not filling in my logbook – enabling me to run longer, cover the distances and make better wages. It went on all the time with drivers. It was wrong. I did it, but I'm not condoning it.

Political correctness just didn't exist, but political extremists were evident in abundance, nowhere more so than in the docklands. I'd been brought up as 'working class', but as a driver I, like just about every other lorry driver, was treated like shit by the dockers.

They were bolshie bastards, with Tilbury Docks the worst of the lot. To say they were lazy, thieving bully boys would be an understatement. They ruled the roost for years – really nasty pieces of work – looking after themselves and not giving a fuck about anybody else. Nobody – nobody – was more pleased than me, when the power of the unions finally crumbled and the dockers got their comeuppance.

On one occasion I was making an early drop at Tilbury. I rolled up just as the dockers were going on their standard one-and-a-half-hour morning break. Can you imagine that in today's world, 90 minutes for breakfast? I watched them all slouch off into this canteen so, rather than sit in the cab like a spare part, I went in for a spot of breakfast myself. As I entered the canteen the cacophony dropped to near silence, quickly followed by murmurings of disgruntlement, rising to downright abuse.

'What the fuck do you think you're doing? This is a 'canteen' for dockers, not drivers. Fuck off out of it.' I got the message. As I was leaving, one of the women who were serving had a quiet word. 'Go round the back and I'll pass something out to you.' It was a kind gesture, even a brave one, considering the venomous nature of her more malevolent regulars.

I walked to the rear of the cafe, being careful to stay out of sight of the local louts. I had to climb up a stack of rickety pallets to reach the kitchen window. I tapped on the pane. The lady opened it and handed me a bacon roll and a coffee. Putting her finger to her lips, she gave me strict orders to stay shtum!

When the thuggish dockers ambled back to work and unloaded the wagon, it was as if nothing had happened. I suppose intimidating behaviour, and ganging up on individuals who were just trying to earn a day's corn, was normal behaviour in their book.

They'd be at their most threatening when I was delivering booze or car parts. It was guaranteed that my wagon wouldn't be unloaded until after dusk. I could arrive at nine o'clock in the morning but it made no difference. It had to be nightfall or late on a winter afternoon, before the thieving bastards would even consider approaching my lorry. Only under the cover of darkness could they siphon off the alcohol, or nick whole pallets of car parts. It was demeaning and bloody frustrating. It was perfectly obvious what they were doing. I knew it, they knew it and whoever was supposed to be in charge of the docks knew it. They were a law unto themselves. Nobody had the balls to do anything about it.

I'd hear bottles being smashed as boxes of gin were 'accidentally' dropped. They'd use the box as a sieve to contain all the broken glass and then drain the booze into kettles, bottles and buckets. It wasn't subtle. It was even more blatant with the car parts. They'd just cart whole pallet loads off into the night, never to be seen again.

I also had the misfortune of several trips to Liverpool, where the dockers were notoriously left wing. I drove up from Kent on at least four occasions carrying air conditioning units destined for Chile. At that time, Chile was under the rule of a right-wing military junta. The bone idle Scousers refused to handle any of the cargo, claiming it was a political protest. Any excuse not to work. Those air conditioners went to and fro between Kent and Merseyside more times than I'd care to remember. Away from the toxicity of the docklands, my time as a lorry driver wasn't all bad, not by any means. When you share a way of life with thousands of others, it's inevitable a sense of camaraderie builds up, and so it was with HGV drivers. It was a brotherhood of a kind, and when the chips were down, we'd come through for each other.

That was certainly true when my truck conked out in roadworks on the M6, en route to Warrington. The timing shaft had gone and it took all week to get it fixed. I hadn't banked on being away for four nights and my money soon ran out. I finally set off back to Maidstone on the Friday afternoon. It was going to be a long trip, entailing an overnight stop at Toddington Services. Demoralised and virtually penniless, apart from the price of a cup of tea, I went into the restaurant area. I bought my solitary cup of tea.

'Are you not eating tonight?' The query came from one of a group of drivers working for Husks, a haulage company in Dover.

'I can't afford it. I've been broken down all week and I'm out of money,' was my response.

'Well, that's no good, is it? Don't worry, son, you're eating with us tonight.' They all clubbed together and bought me a dinner. I was ravenous and so bloody grateful. Not only did they make sure I was fed, they also offered to escort me – convoy style – down to Maidstone, just in case the wagon broke down again. 'We're heading off at 6.30am. If you can leave with us we'll make sure you get home and then we'll push on to Dover.'

I was overwhelmed by such a tremendous gesture to a fellow driver who was down on his luck. The romanticism of the knights of the road was alive and kicking. I was so glad of it that night. It's what I'd signed up for when I achieved that HGV Class 1 licence.

But as other aspects of my life began to develop – namely my relationship with Gina, the woman with whom I'd spend the rest of my life – the cons of being a long distance lorry driver were rapidly outweighing the pros.

I finally reached the end of the road with J&L Smith on a bitterly cold night in November 1977. I was parked up at The Red Lion in Northampton. It was bloody freezing, real brass monkey weather. I woke up at 2am dying for a pee. I opened the cab, absolutely busting. At that very moment, my pillow fell out of the cab and I ended up pissing all over it. What the fuck?

I was half asleep, barely lucid, and then the wall of cold air hit me like a sledgehammer. What was I doing? Why was I living like this? There had to be a better way. I just wanted to be sleeping in my own bed every night with the woman I loved. How could I make it happen?

A guy called Kevin Coomber worked for a courier company called Inter County Express, just down the road from the J&L Smith yard. I'd see him most weeks when he'd make pick-ups from our warehouse. We were chatting one morning when opportunity knocked. 'I probably won't see you again, mate, I'm leaving Inter County next week.'

'Where are you going?' I asked.

'I'm taking a Government course to be a carpenter. I fancy a change and figure I might be good at it.'

'How much do Inter County pay?' I said, sensing an opening. He told me. It was very good money, especially for local work. I've never been one to look a gift horse in the mouth so I went straight round and enquired about the job. I had a chat with the depot manager, Keith Cain, a nice guy, down from Ramsbottom in Lancashire. He seemed to like what I had to say, and I liked what they had to offer. He gave me the job.

I jacked in J&L Smith and my 40-foot wagon, to go and drive what I called a 'Puddle Jumper' – a seven-and-a-half-ton rigid truck. I was entering the world of multi-drop parcels, a business which, by and large, would occupy the rest of my working life.

I started at Inter County assuming I had a new job – why wouldn't I? I'd had the interview with the depot manager and been told I'd got the driving job. It came as a bit of an unwelcome surprise when this guy came up to me and announced, 'I'm the driving assessor. I'll be assessing you today and, depending on my report, you'll either get the job on a permanent basis or not.' What the hell was that all about?

I was scheduled to go to Hastings – about an hour's drive from Maidstone. I'd deliver up to 30 consignments before the hour-long return trip. If this silly sod thought I was going to do all that, only to be told I wasn't getting the job, he was badly mistaken. I had other ideas. I knew I was more than capable of doing the job.

'I'll tell you what I'm going to do. I'm going to drive the four miles to the Jungle Caf, you can do what you've got to do, and when we get there you can tell me if I've got the job or not. I'm not driving all the way to Hastings only for you to tell me, 'No, you're not up to it'.'

I drove to the Jungle Caf on the A20 and turned to the assessor, 'Well?' It was heavily rhetorical.

'Oh, I think you'll pass,' he said. 'Yes, I thought so,' I replied confidently.

My career in express parcels was underway, and with it the creature comforts of going home every night to be with Gina.

6

Georgina and marriage

It wasn't love at first sight. What it was – and still is – is a love everlasting, spanning five decades and still going strong. Marrying Georgina Mary Vincent was the best thing I've ever done. I first met her in 1974; she was just 18 years old and I was 22. We shared the same taste in music – soul and reggae – and we'd dance and 'smooch' many a night away at the Hilltop club in Wrotham. We'd go on dates, out for meals and generally spend time together. Gina always says lust was the attraction. Who am I to argue? We were good together, we hit it off, but I wasn't ready to settle down. I had a hard-earned and well-deserved reputation as 'a player'. I wasn't willing to revoke that status. Inevitably, we drifted apart and, at the time, it wasn't that much of a big deal.

Two years later, I was incredibly fortunate to get a second chance. Lady Luck must've been smiling on me as I drove my 'artic' wagon down the London Road in Maidstone. I spotted Gina and her friend Carole walking to work. When I look back, I shudder to think how close I came to letting her slip away. Had it not been for that chance encounter we wouldn't be celebrating our Ruby wedding anniversary this year.

I pulled over and asked them if they wanted a lift. Thankfully they did. Gina was as gorgeous as ever and she seemed pleased enough to see me. We hadn't parted on bad terms; she'd known what I was like and just accepted it when we split up. There'd been no great drama, no angry exchanges or lingering acrimony. I still had the cheek of the devil so, as we drove along, I asked Gina for her number. She gave it to me. Great, she must still be interested! Full of self confidence, I rang her, asked her out for a drink and, of course, she said 'yes'. That night we went to the Ropemakers pub in New Hythe, and we've been together ever since.

It was different the second time around. I'd sewn my wild oats. I'd matured. I was ready to enter a serious relationship and give it my all. There was something about Gina – something much more than just the physical attraction – but *bloody hell* there was no doubting that attraction. She was stunning. She told me I was a 'handsome bastard'. We were in agreement. The thing I've always noticed about Gina is that everybody likes her – people immediately warm to her – it's been that way ever since we met. My grandad, my mum and dad, Alan and Sandra, my cousins, all my family and friends, everybody approved of her in a big way. It's me they disapproved of, but I learned to live with it.

My driving meant I was 'rationed' to only seeing Gina two or three times a week. This knight of the road caper, with regular overnight runs, was beginning to wear thin. I'd be off to Leeds delivering consignments of paper, onward to Wiles Fertilisers in Beverley and then back south, laden with fertiliser for Kent's farmers. Next I'd be back up to Yorkshire dropping off more paper, before driving west to Crossfield Chemicals in Warrington, picking up a load and finally heading for home. The money was good and Gina and I were growing ever closer, despite the demands of the job keeping us apart.

Calling time on J&L Smith and switching to Inter County Express was a watershed moment in our relationship. It meant I could see Gina just about every night of the week. She was renting a house with her friends Carole and Janet in Coxheath, a small village just outside Maidstone. I'd spend most nights with

Gina, which often prompted Mum to ask, 'Where've you been all week?'

'I've been at Gina's.'

'No you haven't. Gina's a good girl, she wouldn't allow that,' retorted my mum. Gina was certainly good to me and she allowed a lot of things. She couldn't get enough of me, or me her. Mum once said to her, 'What the hell are you doing with him? You could do far better.' She wasn't often wrong, but she was wrong on that one.

But what she'd said in a semi jocular fashion was a more serious issue for Gina's mother, Marie. She was genuinely apprehensive about her daughter dating, and ultimately wanting to marry me. From her perspective she probably thought she had good reason – I was already married. Not only married, but I had a young son. I'd separated from my wife, Jackie, long before Gina came onto the scene. Gina was no marriage-wrecker – that ship had sailed years beforehand.

Jackie was pregnant when we married in a low-key, registry office affair in 1970. She was 17 and I was 19 – not much more than kids ourselves. We were young and stupid and the marriage was more or less doomed to failure from the start. All that was missing from the ceremony was the sound of shotguns!

What was and wasn't socially acceptable in the 1970s is a world and half a century away from 2019. We weren't suffocated by the 'political correctness gone mad' culture of today but, perversely, there was a stricter moral code, one that dictated you did 'the right thing', especially if a girl fell pregnant outside of marriage.

With just an hour or so to go before my wedding, I was in the Queen's Head pub with my grandad, the man I'd so admired as a boy growing up in Kirkcaldy, the man who had influenced my character and outlook on life when I was an infant. He was worldly wise, a realist, a man prepared to give a two-fingered salute to 'doing the right thing'. He handed me a £10 note and told me to get a one-way train ticket out of Maidstone. He knew I was about to make a mistake. Deep down, I knew it too, but it wasn't the right thing to do. Getting married to Jackie was the only course of action.

Sure enough, the marriage didn't last five minutes and we soon parted. Our son, Simon, was born in 1971. Jackie ended up living in Folkestone, whereas I remained in Snodland. I'd drive down every fortnight on a Friday evening to collect Simon, spend the weekend with him and then take him back on the Sunday night. Mum and Dad used to dote on him and spoil him something rotten.

Over a period of weeks and months it became apparent something wasn't right; in fact, things were pretty bad. Jackie was mixing with the wrong type of people and getting into drugs. It wasn't a good environment for a young child. Simon would say things to Mum and Dad – in the innocent ways kids do – but it was enough to alert them to what seemed to be going on.

Eventually it reached the point where Mum put her foot down. She wasn't happy about Simon being in unhealthy, who knows, even potentially dangerous, surroundings. She wanted him to be safe and in a stable home. Mum and Dad wanted to raise Simon. More tellingly, Simon wanted to live with them in Snodland.

'If you want to bring him up, it's your decision, but he'll be your responsibility, not mine,' I told Mum. It sounded brutal, but it was time for straight talking, and that was the truth. Jackie descended deeper into the drugs scene and Simon came to live with Mum and Dad. He basically benefited from the same upbringing as I'd had with Cathie and Charlie Bell. The only bit missing was the hardship of living on the poverty line.

Throughout all the trauma and emotional turbulence of Simon's situation, Gina had been incredibly supportive and understanding. It was a lot for a young woman to take on, but by now we were committed to each other. This was the real deal. We decided to put our relationship to the test. We'd have a sunshine holiday in one of my favourite haunts and, if we were happy to be with one another 24/7 for a fortnight, we'd get engaged. We were heading for Malta.

Five years after I'd first fallen in love with the country, sandwiched between Sicily and the North African coast, I was now sharing it with the woman I loved. Admittedly my food and drinks weren't being subsidised by German tourists this time around, but we had a great time. We soaked up the Mediterranean sun on the beaches and in the beautiful secluded coves. We hired a Mini (unfortunately it cost more than eight packets of grommets) and I showed Gina the whole island.

My standout memory of that holiday wasn't the best. We were staying in Birzebbuga, a quaint fishing village near Marsaxlokk Bay, on the southern tip of the country. On the day in question we'd gone on a day out to Gozo – an island off the north coast of Malta.

Geographically, we were more than 4,000 miles away from the Indian capital, but I was struck down with 'Delhi belly' like never before. It was 90-degree heat and I had 'the shits' virtually non-stop. The return trip was a nightmare. What began as stomach gripes while waiting for the ferry quickly escalated into the worst bout of food poisoning I'd ever experienced.

I spent the entire voyage in the loo. I ran out of toilet paper and was reduced to wiping my arse with lollipop sticks and wrappers – it was horrendous. How I managed to get back to our apartment without having an 'accident' I will never know. The only good thing to emerge from the nightmare incident was Gina had seen me in sickness as well as in health. It would bode well for our marriage vows. We were getting hitched.

At this point I'll confess, I've never been the biggest romantic in the world, but I'd still dispute Gina's recollection of why I proposed. She reckons I asked her to marry me because of the tax breaks given to married couples. I've always been good with numbers, but surely even I wasn't that crass?

Irrespective of the how, what and why, we were due to get engaged on a Saturday in September 1978. I had to work at the Inter County depot until lunchtime and then I needed to put a new clutch into my Ford Cortina. I knocked off at midday, and me and my mate, Tony, spent the afternoon under this bloody Cortina. It was bitch of a job and I didn't arrive home until about 4pm, covered in grease and oil.

My first words to Gina were, 'Sorry, George, we can't get engaged today, it's too late now and I'm filthy.' She wasn't having any of it. 'Get yourself in that bath. We'll get you cleaned up – we're bloody well getting engaged and we're getting engaged today.' I was duly scrubbed from head to toe and we made a mad dash into Maidstone before H. Samuel the Jewellers closed.

If we bought Gina's engagement ring on that particular day, we'd benefit from a special offer where we'd get the wedding rings for some ridiculously cheap price. We made it in time and the ring was duly purchased. So there we were, an engaged couple, but no party, no pomp or ceremony.

It soon became apparent that Gina would be denied a traditional 'white' wedding in the Canterbury diocese. As a divorcee I was persona non grata in the eyes of the Church of England, a fact made very clear by the vicar of St Mary's in Frittenden – Gina's local church. It was almost as if he was revelling in the moment when he told me, 'I can't marry you, Tom. You've been married before, and it's strictly forbidden for me to allow a divorced person to marry another person in my church. It's simply not permitted in the diocese of Canterbury.'

I lost my rag with the sanctimonious man of the cloth, told him he was being an arsehole and walked away. I wasn't that fussed about a church wedding, but it was what Gina wanted and I was angry that she was going to be denied her 'big day'.

We tried again, this time at All Saints' Church, in Staplehurst, in the hope of a more liberal and enlightened approach. As soon as Gina and I sat down with Reverend Vickery I knew we were onto a winner. We were perched on a settee at the vicarage opposite the vicar. I could see trays of beer cans under his chair. I thought 'this is my kind of clergyman'.

I was right. Rev Vickery reiterated that, although diocese rules meant he wasn't allowed to wed us in church, he would happily preside over a blessing ceremony, complete with an exchanging of vows. It was the closest thing he could muster to a bona fide church wedding. We happily agreed and the date was set – October 27th 1979.

We married at the local registry office in Maidstone in the morning. Our friends, Des and Lesley Bailey, acted as witnesses, as well as best man and bridesmaid. The blessing took place in the afternoon, followed by the reception, party and disco at Frittenden Village Hall, aided and abetted by The Bell & Jorrocks – the local pub.

The reception was very much a DIY affair. We couldn't afford professional caterers, so the food was cooked and prepared by family and friends. We had homemade soup (an upgrade on the 1950s' Kirkcaldy version) as the starter, a ham salad for the mains, followed by some kind of dessert, I can't remember what. It wasn't elaborate but it suited us, and our guests and everybody enjoyed themselves. It was a good 'do'. We did however make one big mistake with the seating plan – we sat my grandad next to the vicar!

The pair of them got on like a house on fire – probably ignited by the whisky fumes – as they demolished not one, but two, bottles of Scotland's finest. Rev Vickery was due to conduct a service at Maidstone Prison on the Saturday evening. He never made it. We had to carry him out of the village hall and back to the vicarage. He didn't save any souls that night – the spirits had very much got the better of him.

Whisky would also be on the menu as we headed for our 'honeymoon suite' at the Greenways Hotel – a 45-minute drive away, near Brands Hatch. British Summertime was drawing to a close so we'd gain an extra hour in bed – not a bad thing on your wedding night.

The fog was coming down, so the new Mrs Bell and I left our guests and the ongoing celebrations at around 8.30pm. I drove – I'd hardly touched a drop of alcohol all day – and when we arrived we both fancied something to eat. It was 9.15pm.

The head barman informed us that The Grill had closed at 9pm. There was zero chance of any hot food. It was our wedding night and we were both bloody starving. The best the hotel could do was give us a large bag of crisps – I thought, *Bloody hell, don't overdo it!* Luckily, I'd taken a bottle of whisky from the wedding reception, so there we were, in bed, eating crisps, drinking whisky and, would you believe, I had Match of the Day on the TV? Who said romance was dead?

The next day we moved into our first proper home together – a two-bedroom, semi-detached in Veles Road, Snodland. We didn't have a honeymoon; our money had gone into the house.

Nine months later I would come home and break the news we were moving to Southampton. It marked a period of fundamental change in our lives. I was progressing well with TNT (the Australian-based parcels company had bought Inter County Express in 1978) and taking the promotion was a no-brainer. The dilemma revolved around Simon.

He was 10-years old, doing well at school and was very settled with Mum and Dad. They insisted they wanted to continue bringing him up. It seemed like the right decision. If he'd come with us he'd have had to adapt to a whole new way of life. It could've been very difficult and unnecessarily disruptive for him. Looking back, I can't help but wonder if taking him to Southampton would've altered our relationship, made it stronger and more fruitful? We're estranged nowadays. We haven't been in contact for a number of years. It's regrettable, but it's just the way it is. Things don't always turn out as you would wish.

In every other aspect, Southampton was good for us. I was laying the foundations for future managerial success with TNT, and on June 1st 1984 our son, Scott, was born. Gina had given up work to be a full-time mum. She was happy in Hampshire.

Just three months after becoming a mum I was to tell Gina we'd be on the move once again. I'd accepted another promotion and was on my way to work at TNT's UK & Ireland headquarters.

All roads led to Atherstone in Warwickshire. Gina was, as always, incredibly supportive. She looked after the home and I looked after the wage packet.

I switched to the Head Office in the September. I was determined that Gina and I wouldn't be parted for a day longer than was absolutely necessary. Gina and Scott moved up to the Midlands on December 10th. It'd taken me three months to get us all back together again – it was a good result. As my status within TNT grew, so too did the demands on my time. The irony wasn't lost on Gina or myself as I began spending increasingly long periods away from home. If absence really did make the heart grow fonder, we'd have a quarter of a century to put that theory to the test.

In years to come, I'd be visiting depots, addressing conferences, attending board meetings, speaking at seminars – all manner of things. I'd be flying all over the globe on business trips, to the USA, Australia and Asia. It was light years removed from jacking in my job at J&L Smith to spend more time with my girlfriend. They call it 'progress'.

My daughter Amy and my wonderful grandchildren Felix and Lily Marie

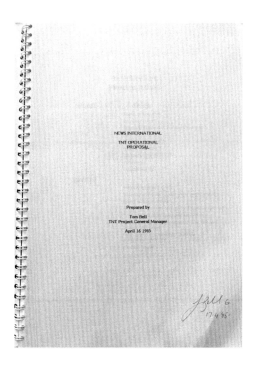

TNT's 'Wapping' proposal to News International. Only a dozen copies were produced. I kept Number 6.

My grandad Tam and his horse Billy on the Kirkcaldy coal round.

Luka Modric, FIFA & UEFA Player of the Year 2018, with me during his time at my beloved Spurs.

Proudest moment of my life as Her Majesty The Queen presented me with the OBE.

An Officer of the Most Excellent Order of the British Empire
– what an honour.

Me and the red Triumph Herald that served us so well in Malta in 1973.

Reflecting on success in the TNT Boardroom.

Me and Bono. When it came to money and taxes I thought the U2 singer was a hypocrite.

Me (right), my brother Alan and my sister Sandra back in the day.

I had a tough, but happy, upbringing in Kirkcaldy.

Our wedding day. Now, 40 years on, Gina and I are still going strong.

Me, The Duke of Edinburgh, TNT Company Secretary, Gerry Ginty, his wife Anne and Gina at one of the numerous occasions when I sat down with Royalty.

The Princess Royal opened TNT's new headquarters at Atherstone. I'm pictured with Alan Jones (left), Les Williams and Stan Dalton (right) during Princess Anne's visit.

7

Genius or madman?

'Who the fuck are you?' I asked as the passenger door swung open and this bloke stuck his head inside my Inter County Express truck. 'You'll find out soon enough who I am, don't you worry, lad,' came the reply in a broad Lancastrian accent. 'Well, what the fuck are you doing?' 'I'm checking your water bottle levels for your windscreen wipers,' said the mysterious intruder.

It wasn't the most conventional way of addressing the boss of my new employers, but that's how it played out on a winter afternoon at our Maidstone depot. I'd pulled in to refuel at the diesel pump, and I was swearing at Bill Hanley, the director and principal driving force behind Inter County. He would become a lifelong friend, a mentor and an influential figure in what could justifiably be described as my 'meteoric rise' through the ranks of TNT. Astute, blunt and indefatigable, Bill worked long, long hours, striving tirelessly to build and enhance his parcel company's reputation. Having served in the RAF, Bill left the armed forces in 1952 and bought a five-tonne truck, delivering coal as a self-employed driver. In some aspects, Bill's rise to the top was not dissimilar to mine. We began life behind the wheel of a lorry, shifted through the metaphorical gears and went all the way to the boardroom.

Bill had been a driver, a foreman, a traffic operator and transport manager before working his way up to senior managerial positions. He played an integral role in the founding of Inter County Express, formed by the amalgamation of two transportation companies from the North West of England – Knowles Vanlines and Dickinsons Transport of Rossendale.

Just like me, he was a man from humble origins. Just like me, he would go on to receive Royal recognition from Buckingham Palace. Bill was made a Member of the British Empire (MBE) in 1996 for services to the transport and express delivery industry.

That first 'colourful exchange' with him happened at 5pm on a Friday. He'd have been lucky to get back home to Ramsbottom, Lancashire, much before 10 or 11 o'clock that night. He epitomised all that was good about Inter County – a great guy, never afraid of hard work, a man who'd always see the job through. He embodied the qualities that ultimately attracted TNT to buy Inter County in 1978.

The UK acquisition was a major step in TNT's expansion into international markets in Europe, North America and South America in the 1970s. The company had started in 1946 when Ken Thomas, an Aussie entrepreneur, launched a business comprising one man and one truck. By 1962, Thomas Nationwide Transport (TNT) was listed on the Sydney Stock Exchange. Five years later TNT merged with Alltrans, a privately owned freight transportation company founded by Sir Peter Abeles. It began trading in New Zealand, the first time the company had operated outside of Australia.

As well as being a milestone in the evolution of TNT, 1978 was also a significant year for me, as I moved away from life behind a steering wheel.

I'd only been with Inter County for a few months before TNT bought the firm, but I'd started well. A guy called Tony Sim, the company's Regional General Manager, approached me.

'I want you to work in the office.' I said, 'I can't afford to, Tony,

I'm earning good money.' Unless you were in senior management, blue-collar workers would invariably earn more than their white-collar counterparts.

Tony asked, 'How much are you earning?'

'£5,000 a year,' was my response.

He said, 'I'll give you £6,500 to go and work in that office.'

At this point the negotiations concluded and I swiftly swapped my truck for a desk. I was in bloody heaven. No more nights, no more early starts, no more working in a freezing warehouse, and £1,500 to the good. The office was a wooden cabin at the time, as we were preparing to move to a brand new, 36-door, purpose-built depot in Hall Road, Aylesford. Tony tasked me to go down to the new site and mark out the warehouse space, which I duly did. I drew up the plan and arrived back.

Tony asked, 'Have you done it?'

'Yes,' I said.

'Well, let's have a look, then. You've only used half the space; that's no bloody good,' said Tony.

'It's double what we've got at the moment,' I said, somewhat defensively.

'Go back and do it again. We're going to need all of it, the whole warehouse.' I thought, *He's a bit bloody optimistic*, but he was absolutely right. The parcel volumes went through the roof. Tony clearly knew what he was on about.

Over the next couple of years he'd present me with a myriad of challenges and opportunities. He'd teach me things about the business – sometimes without me even realising – and it'd stand me in great stead for years to come.

Tony must have seen something in me at an early stage and set out to develop my potential. I didn't always see it that way.

He was constantly changing my job. One minute I was Morning Shift Supervisor, the next I'd be Backshift Supervisor or Nightshift Supervisor. I stepped up to be Office Manager and later moved to Traffic Operator. I was gaining insight and experience into the workings of every aspect of the depot with each different role. His 'grand plan' wasn't obvious to me, but it worked.

We duly moved into the new premises. Business was booming. Six months later, it was time for the official depot opening. We would be in safe hands with JPR Williams, the iconic Welsh rugby union international full back, performing the ceremonial honours. Of even more importance, Sir Peter Abeles – the boss of TNT worldwide – would be in attendance.

Tony wanted the depot immaculate for the big day. I was put on gardening duty. I had to lay new turf at the front and the back of the offices. Had Tony heard about my distinction in gardening at Snodland Secondary? The thought crossed my mind. Over the next fortnight I spent hours outside in the warm sunshine grassing up the site.

Everything was on schedule right up until the night before the opening. I was toiling to turf a steep bank of mud – a sheer wall of soil that'd been excavated when the depot was built.

'Simbo', as Tony was known, pulled up in his big red Citroen. He jumped out, 'Is this thing going to be finished in time?' 'I don't know, Tony. I just can't get the turf to stay put. It won't stick, there's no grip, it just keeps sliding off.'

'Stay there!' he boomed and strode off around the corner. Within two minutes Tony was back with a big box of 10-inch nails, 'Nail the buggers on!'

I can guarantee you, if you went down to TNT's Maidstone depot today, you'll still find that turf nailed on.

I could never work out if Tony was a genius or a madman – perhaps he was a bit of both – but there was never a dull moment. He lived life like he drove his car – with his foot to the floor. I was on the loading dock one afternoon when Tony's Citroen zoomed into the yard at 80mph, before screeching to a halt at the back of the depot. He jumped out, up onto the dock, threw his car keys at me and said, 'Fill her up when you've got a minute,' before disappearing into his office. The next minute a police car, blue light flashing, roared into view. Two coppers got out and one said, 'Where is he?'

'Where's who, Officer,' I asked.

'You know who – the fella who drives that bloody thing,' said the copper, pointing at the red Citroen.

'He's in his office. Do you want him?'

'Bloody right we do. Go and get him.' I ran up the stairs to Tony's office. 'Tony, there's two coppers downstairs and they want to see you.'

Simbo went downstairs and, cool as a cucumber, said, 'Yes, Officers, how can I help you?'

'You can help us by explaining why you've just gone past us doing 80mph by the railway station.'

'Me?' said Tony, as if butter wouldn't melt in his mouth. 'I haven't been out the office.'

The copper looked exasperated. 'We've just seen you go hurtling past us!' Tony turned towards me, rolling his eyes towards heaven, pointing at the car keys that were still in my grasp. 'You know how it is, Officers, you give these young guys your car keys and they can't resist having a blast in the boss's car. I'll make sure it doesn't happen again.'

The policemen looked at me, then back to Tony. 'We'll have you. We'll bloody have you. Next time, next time,' they said, shaking their heads, their eyes trained on Simbo. He was a real character. He had my best interests at heart, but he was also unpredictable.

Life was good. I was making a decent fist of running the office and had settled into a comfortable routine. Gina was working for a paper company a mile up the road from the depot. She'd drop me off at 8.30am and return to pick me up at 5.30pm. Everything was running like clockwork.

Gina drove up at half past five one afternoon and Tony stuck his head out of the upstairs office window, 'Sorry, Mrs B, I need to speak to TB; he's going to be late home tonight.' I went up to the office and Tony spouted a load of old rubbish for about an hour before I managed to get away. This happened again on the Tuesday, Wednesday and Thursday – it was ridiculous. I said, 'Tony, this is the fourth night you've called me back and proceeded to talk nonsense – what's going on?'

'What makes you think you've a God-given right to come in here at 8.30am and leave bang on time at 5.30pm every night? You're getting too comfortable. Starting Monday, you're Backshift Supervisor!' Tony sounded pretty pissed off. It came as a bit of a shock, and I wasn't best pleased either.

I went into work at 1pm on the Monday to organise the backshift. I noticed a bright yellow Citroen CV in Tony's parking spot. I assumed his car was in for a service. I was wrong.

He came out of his office, handed me a pair of binoculars, a clipboard and pen and told me to get into the CV. We were heading for Tunbridge on a special 'field operation'. I didn't have a clue what he was on about.

We hit heavy traffic. That didn't deter Tony. He'd planned for all contingencies. He avoided the long queues by driving up and along a rutted grass verge. The Citroen CV didn't have much going for it, but it did have a robust suspension system and was perfect for the job. Simbo then drove straight into a cornfield, hence the yellow car. We'd reached our destination and we were heavily camouflaged. Armed with the binoculars, I was instructed to climb a tree to provide me with a perfect vantage point of a lay-by on the A21. Tony peeled back the sunroof of the CV, proceeding to stand on the back seat and bark his orders through the open-top vehicle.

'Chapman will be along in about 10 minutes' time. I want you to observe him and report back anything and everything he does.' Brian Chapman was one of the depot drivers and his daily run took him to Hastings and back. Typically, he'd make 25 or 26 drops and bring back four or five items which he couldn't deliver.

It was a bizarre sight. There was me up a tree with binoculars, spying on an empty lay-by, whereas Tony, with his head sticking through the roof of the car, held the clipboard, pen poised in the middle of this field.

At 3pm Chapman's van duly parked up in the lay-by. 'Chapman's just arrived,' I shouted. Tony noted the time. I was up that bloody tree for nearly an hour. Nothing happened. Just before 4pm, Chapman started up his engine, flicked on his indicator and pulled out onto the A21.

'He's just pulling out and getting back on the road,' I reported.

'Quick, get down from that tree and get in the car. I want to be back at the depot before Chapman gets back,' said Tony.

Thanks to a crazy return drive to the depot we were back before Chapman. Tony said, 'I want you to debrief him, but without letting on about what we've seen today.' Chapman rolled in at his usual 5pm. I'm ready for him and I can barely suppress a grin. 'Hi, Brian, has it been a tough day?' I asked.

'Yes, I've done 26 drops but had to bring back five.' Tony was standing behind me. I was anticipating Chapman getting the mother of all bollockings. To my astonishment Tony empathised with Chapman. 'Yeah, it's hard for you guys, in and out of the truck, battling your way through traffic. Keep up the good work.'

I was gobsmacked. Why wasn't Chapman being hauled over the coals? This went on all week until Tony said, 'When Chapman gets back send him up to me.' 'It'll be my pleasure,' I said.

Brian came back to the depot bang on 5pm. 'Right, upstairs, Tony wants to see you.' This time I couldn't help myself. A knowing grin spread across my face. I'm thinking Tony's going to hammer him for taking all those hours off in the middle of the afternoon.

Ten minutes later Chapman emerged from Simbo's office. He was positively beaming from ear to ear. I said, 'What've you got to be so happy about?'

'Tony's given me a £5-a-week pay rise and promoted me to being a driving assessor. He reckons if I can do 26 drops a day, have time for breakfast and lunch and spend an hour in a lay-by every day, I could teach the other buggers a thing or two.'

It was another lesson learned. Turn a vice into a virtue. Show people their worth and maximise their talents for the greater good. From that day on Brian never brought another drop back.

On another occasion I'd just finished doing all the routes for the next day's deliveries. We didn't have computers; everything was done on a chalkboard. The schedule showed the name of the driver, the number of the wagon, where it was going and how many drops it was due to make. It was 6.30pm and Tony walked in. 'I'm sorry, but Fleet Numbers 17, 21, 27, 29 and 30 are off the road.' He took the blackboard rubber and wiped them off. 'You'll have to re-route what's left to cover for the five missing wagons.' Oh shit.

I spent the next hour and a half re-jigging everything, allocating extra parcels to other drivers and trying to ensure we could maintain the service levels. Just after 8pm Tony returned. 'How've you got on?'

'I've managed to cover for four of the missing wagons but I'm struggling on the fifth,' I said in an apologetic fashion.

'Well, you'll be pleased to know that all five vehicles are back on the road,' said Simbo in a triumphant tone.

'How's that happened?' I queried. 'They were all out of commission less than two hours ago.'

Tony had put me to the test and I just about passed it with flying colours. He said, 'Just because you've 30 vehicles at your disposal doesn't mean you have to use all 30 – think of vehicle productivity and efficiency.' It was a lesson which stuck with me and one that was especially handy when I was promoted to Operations Manager at Southampton.

Simbo was a real character but nowadays he'd never get away with some of the things he used to do. I considered myself pretty savvy and streetwise, but Tony was on a different level. I always tried to keep on his right side – quite literally – and for good reason.

Every day I'd accompany Tony and depot Operations Manager, Neil Crossthwaite, on a walk around the warehouse. It was the equivalent of the early morning team meeting, only it took place on foot instead of sitting down in Tony's office. Simbo had nicknames for us both. Neil was 'Blunders One' and I was 'Blunders Two'.

Poor old Neil would often fall foul of Tony's unorthodox management style on our walkabout sessions. Simbo would quiz him on operational matters. If Blunders One didn't come up with the right answer there'd be swift and violent consequences. Tony would react by grabbing him by the lapels and throwing him to the left.

If the loading bay shutters were down, Neil would hit them. If the shutters were up and a trailer was parked on the dock, Neil would end up in the back of the trailer.

The worst-case scenario would be the shutters were up, there'd be no trailer in the bay and Neil would go crashing down to the yard a few feet below. How he never suffered a serious injury is beyond me. Tony's methods were unconventional to say the least. It was wrong, but there was no malicious intent.

With hindsight, there may even have been method behind the madness. Blunders One and Blunders Two didn't do too badly as a result of Tony's tutelage. We both went on to become managing directors – Neil at TNT Logistics and me at TNT Express Delivery Services.

One day in August 1980, Tony asked me a question right out of the blue, 'Do you want to be an Operations Manager?' Did I want to be an Operations Manager? Too bloody right I did. The job came with a brand new company car, and my old banger was falling apart.

'Yes, I'd love to be Ops Manager. Why?'

'Right,' said Tony, 'you've a choice of either Southampton or Cannock; which one do you want?'

My response came in an instant. 'Well I'm not moving to the bloody Midlands.'

'It'll be Southampton for you, then,' said Simbo.

8

Up for the fight

I've always led by example. I've never asked anybody to do something I couldn't or wouldn't be prepared to do myself. I've never shied away from a challenge in the work environment, never been afraid to face up to those who would seek to beat me down. I've never let caution temper my natural instinct to take risks, never blinked first when going eye-to-eye with an adversary. I've never lacked self belief. Had I done so I would never have made it to the very top in a high-octane, fast-moving business sector.

I'd gratefully accepted the promotion as Operations Manager at Southampton, the pay rise, the company car and the loan of a TNT wagon to move my furniture and worldly goods down from Snodland. I was told, in no uncertain terms, that if I failed to make the grade there was no safety net, no going back into my comfort zone, no easy return to the Maidstone depot. I had to gamble on my abilities and impress the hell out of everybody.

It was only my second day in the new job when I unexpectedly put down a personal marker that I meant business. The TNT articulated lorry rolled up at the depot's diesel pump. The driver jumped out and started refuelling. I was on the loading dock and called out, 'When you've finished filling her up, put your trailer on here please.'

He shouted back, 'The yard's too narrow. Get a couple of other trailers shifted out of the way first, and then I'll back it on.' The 'artic' drivers were the crème de la crème of TNT's driving 'corps'. They were looked up to and respected by all the other drivers. Many of those who drove the small vans and the 7.5 rigid trucks aspired to be behind the wheel of an 'artic', complete with a HGV Class 1 licence under their belt.

I jumped off the dock, walked over to the fuelling station and asked the driver for the ignition key. The guy was a bit surprised, but he handed me the keys to his wagon. I climbed up into the cab and backed the trailer straight on to the loading bay – a textbook manoeuvre.

'Now, don't you ever tell me you can't put a trailer on this dock!' Suitably chastised, the driver offered nothing by way of verbal resistance. Actions spoke louder than words. The story spread like wildfire. The new Ops Manager wasn't taking any shit.

A few days later the home phone rang at 1am. It was a call from the Nightshift Supervisor, a guy called Harry. 'Is that Tom Bell, the Operations Manager?' came the query down the line.

'Yes it is. What's the problem?'

'The backshift haven't left us any milk for the lads' tea break. What am I going to do?'

I said, 'Leave it to me, I'll sort it.'

I got dressed, went downstairs, got a pint of milk out of the fridge and drove to the depot. I met Harry and gave him the bottle of milk. I also gave him the sack. If he couldn't organise a cup of tea and a pint of milk, he was no bloody good to me as a supervisor of men. Harry's mate, Dennis, saw the writing on the wall. He asked me to get him a move to Exeter depot as a driver, which I did.

I recruited new supervisors, Dave Potter and Ivan Buckle, younger men who were open to new ideas, eager to graft and adaptable to a different approach. This was the TNT way. I had no time for weak-willed, bumbling buffoons. By contrast, I was blessed with a superb bunch of delivery drivers – outstanding individuals who took immense pride in their work – who made my job a whole lot easier. They were all first rate, and three live long in my memory.

Geoff Cooley had 130 drops on his Portsmouth run – a helluva lot – so I took 40 off his route and spread the load across other drivers. The next morning Geoff went ballistic. 'I'll tell you when I want drops taken off me for Pompey,' he protested. The next day he went out armed with 125 deliveries and cleared the lot. Ian Black would make 100 deliveries per day in Bournemouth, whereas Ian Jull would have no problems doing 70 drops a day over in Weymouth. Productivity levels were excellent and the new job was going like a dream, but my days as Operations Manager were numbered.

I'd only been at Southampton for two months when I was promoted to Depot Manager. The gamble – if it had ever been a gamble – had paid off handsomely. I was reaping the dividends at work, but paying a high price on the domestic front. I was away from home six nights a week, Sunday to Friday. I had to work Saturday mornings, which meant travelling back to Snodland on the Saturday afternoons. No sooner was I home with Gina, and I'd be back down to Southampton late on a Sunday, ready for the Monday morning start-up. I was a 'victim' of my own success.

My reputation was on the rise and my profile within the company was getting noticed. I was handed the proverbial poisoned chalice, the antithesis of Southampton. I was directed to go and sort out the malcontents and growing mayhem at TNT Milton in Oxfordshire.

I was pitched into my first major battle with bolshie workers who were dictating what could and couldn't happen at the depot and generally taking the piss out the business. I wasn't due to start my troubleshooting role until the Monday morning but decided to travel up on the Saturday.

Tachograph technology was just coming in at the time and Milton's fleet was being fitted with the new driver safety equipment.

The kit would gather data on the driver's hours, how far he'd driven within a stipulated timeframe, where he'd gone, the speed of the lorry. It was the stuff that would've been the bane of my life and stunted my earning capacity back in the days of J&L Smith. That said, it was the right thing to be happening, especially since it no longer impacted on my wage packet. The tachographs were being fitted into the vehicles at Milton depot but had to be calibrated at an independent garage – authorised by the Department of Transport – at Botley, 10 miles away.

I arrived at Milton, introduced myself and said I'd drive one of the wagons to the calibration centre. The depot staff looked at me in astonishment. 'They won't like you doing that,' I was told. 'Who won't like me doing what?' I queried. I already knew the answer.

'The union – they won't want you driving the truck.'

'I don't care what they like,' I said, and climbed up into the cab. I had a welcome committee waiting at the other end, led by the Senior Shop Steward, a guy called Cyril Trinder. His first words to me were, 'Management are not allowed to drive the trucks!' My reaction was less than conciliatory. 'Get this in your head. Management will decide who's driving the fucking trucks and I'm driving that one,' I said, pointing to the wagon I'd just driven up from Milton.

'I'll be taking it back and then I'll bring another one up, and I'll take that one back as well. Got it?' Cyril and his union brothers were powerless to stop me, but they didn't like it, they didn't like it one bit. Word reached me later that day: the union was convening a meeting outside the depot gates at 11.30am on Sunday. It was a direct result of my 'provocative' action. I decided to attend.

As I approached the depot gates, I was told, 'This is a union meeting for union members only.'

'Fair enough,' I said, producing my fully paid up Transport & General Workers Union membership card from my pocket. 'I don't have a problem with it being union members only. I'll be staying.'

The meeting organisers looked at each other and then they looked at me. They didn't have a clue what to do. The whole thing fell apart and they all drifted off to the pub. I hadn't even officially started at Milton, but by the Monday morning they were all aware of me. They were pulling all kinds of Spanish practices; management weren't allowed in the warehouse, drivers were picking up £1.20 instead of 20p per collection of any unscheduled parcel pick-ups. Even the cleaner was trying it on, trying to wangle more money than her agreed rate.

One of my first moves was to promote a troublesome shop steward – Gerry Barber – to Traffic Operator. From that day to this, I've never seen a more dramatic transformation of poacher turned gamekeeper. That completely wrong-footed the union faction, but they were still up for a fight. A number of militants were running more than 10 minutes late returning from a lunch break. I went into the canteen. 'Come on, you lot, back to work.'

'Fuck off, we've seen off better than you,' came a rebellious voice.

'Really?' I replied. 'Well, you've never seen the likes of me before, now get back to work.'

Then they started. They'd be working 'go slows' on different shifts over each 24-hour period. The morning shift would work as usual, the backshift would go slow. The night shift would operate normally and the morning shift would go slow. The backshift would work properly and then the nightshift would go slow. It went on all week. I'll admit, by Friday afternoon I was knackered. I'd been on my feet, fire-fighting almost non-stop. I was ready to go home for the weekend.

The Milton Depot General Manager, Ron McDonald, appeared after lunch. 'Is everything alright, Tom?' It was a rhetorical question from his perspective.

'I'm shattered, Ron. I've been on my feet all week. I'll be glad to get home.'

Ron seemed surprised. 'Why? What's the matter? What've you been up to?'

'What have I been up to? You've effectively had four days of strike action this week, didn't you know?' If I sounded exasperated it's because I was.

'No. Things seemed to be going OK. I haven't seen any problems,' said the GM. Talk about not knowing if you were having a shit, shave or a haircut, he had no idea what was going on in his own depot. There was a war of attrition being waged and my 'General' was bloody clueless as to where the battle lines were drawn.

One of the turning points came in the middle of the night during the depths of winter. It was 3am and I was in my office which overlooked the warehouse.

I was in conversation with one of the younger lads who worked on the loading dock. I wanted to know why he thought morale was so low in the depot and the sense of grievance so high? Gazing out of my window onto the shop floor he said, 'Just look at it, it's like a prison.'

I was intrigued, 'How do you mean, it's like a prison?'

'Well, there are wire cage dividers on every loading bay, the metal shutters are always up, it's cold and soulless. It's just a horrible place to work.'

I took the lad's feedback at face value. I ordered the removal of all the wire bay dividers, ensured the shutters were only open when necessary and arranged for the installation of a radio system on the shop floor. The change was remarkable. The improvements were a catalyst for an upturn in morale. I'd fought and won the running battles with the union members, but I'd also listened to their perceptions of the depot. After nine months of slogging up and down from Southampton to Milton and back, I'd finally cracked it. The drive to and from work took a total of three hours each day (it was before the Newbury by-pass) and meant I left home at 6am and returned at 9pm. It wasn't sustainable. I was on the verge of putting my house on the market and moving to Oxfordshire when I received a phone call offering me the position of General Manager at Southampton. Hallelujah!

9

Born leader

It was a Saturday morning. The phone rang. My hands were covered in sticky tile adhesive. I was tiling the kitchen at home in Hythe. I wasn't doing a great job of it. The interruption was a blessing in disguise.

'Good morning, Tom, Alan here. What's your RPC?' The caller was Alan Jones, Managing Director of TNT UK.

He wanted to know if I knew the Revenue per Consignment – the amount of money generated for each consignment – at TNT's Southampton depot. I was taking up my new position as the depot General Manager in less than 48 hours.

'I don't know. I don't start the job until Monday,' was my caught off guard reply.

'Who's your biggest customer?'

'I'm not sure, Alan. I've a good idea who it is, but I'm not sure,' I said, trying not to lose too much credibility.

'Make sure you find out before Monday!' End of phone call.

Bloody hell, I hadn't even started the job and I was already being grilled by the boss.

I spent most of Sunday rooting around the office, sifting through files and paperwork, getting the answers. Monday came and went. Alan didn't call. Tuesday morning the phone jangled into life on my desk. It was the man I'd grow to admire and respect and with whom I'd forge a formidable and hugely successful business double act – it was 'The Jones'.

I had all the answers, just like Alan knew I would. He had as much faith in my abilities as I had.

In the mid-80s and throughout the 1990s, we'd be crucial to the organic growth of TNT, as the company became the most profitable in the British express delivery industry. We were a potent combination, one that blazed a trail for others to follow. When Alan was given the job of steering TNT's worldwide operations and fortunes, I would succeed him as MD of the business in the UK & Ireland.

General management was a job I was born to do. I was in my element. I loved it. I'd be in work at 7.30am to see the C&D (*Collection* & *Delivery*) drivers go out, and I wouldn't go home until I'd seen them all back in. They were my drivers, just like the loading bank operatives (those who'd load and unload the parcels on and off the wagons) were my guys, and the admin and sales team were my people – it was as if I was running my own business, with Hampshire and Dorset as my domain.

I took such pride in seeing my fleet on the road. I was surrounded with excellent staff, professional to the core, all striving to be the best they could possibly be. Sometimes I'd drive the long way round to work, taking in the New Forest and all the beautiful countryside. If that didn't set a man up for a working day, I don't know what would. These were the best of times and they were about to get even better.

As Depot Manager, and later as General Manager, I'd shown I knew what it took to generate healthy revenue streams and good profit margins. I was, however, still something of a novice in the sponsorship stakes. An opportunity presented itself via Hampshire County Cricket Club. Instinctively, I wanted to go into bat for TNT Southampton, but I needed the go-ahead and funding from Head Office.

As chance would have it, I was up for a budget review meeting in Atherstone the following week. I was in the gents' toilet when Adam Shuter, the Marketing Manager, walked in. I managed to dispel the myth that men can't multi-task, by continuing to pee, while telling Adam about the approach from the cricket club. It was a season-long, shirt sponsorship deal in a newly-launched one-day cricket Sunday competition – the John Player League. 'What do you reckon?' I asked, expecting an instant knock-back.

'How much are we talking about?'

'Around £12,000 to £13,000,' I said.

'Go for it. Find out what they're offering and we'll see what we can do,' said Adam, as our impromptu meeting came to a close.

Hampshire were already a big draw in English cricket, boasting two legends from the West Indies – batsman, Gordon Greenidge, and demon fast bowler, Malcolm Marshall. Hampshire's Commercial Manager Mike Taylor outlined the package: a marquee with running buffet and free bar, catering for up to 120 customers at four fixtures in strategic locations, namely Portsmouth, Southampton, Bournemouth and Basingstoke. Head Office gave it the green light.

A few weeks later I was standing in an empty marquee in Portsmouth looking at the vast quantities of food and booze laid out on the tables. It was 11am on the Sunday. I was nervous. The 'open invitation' to TNT's customers told them the buffet and refreshments began at 12.30pm and ran all day.

The cricket was secondary for me. I wanted customers – lots of customers – enjoying themselves and thinking, believing, that TNT was the dog's bollocks.

I shouldn't have worried. It was packed to the rafters. Talk about speculate to accumulate. It was the same at Basingstoke and Bournemouth, whereas Southampton was just ridiculous – massively oversubscribed as the sponsorship paid back in spades. The Tristar revenue leapt from £15,000 to £20,000 per week, a big return on investment. I renewed the deal with Hampshire the following season and revenues were running at £23,000 per week. My instincts had paid off handsomely. John Ovens, the Divisional General Manager for the Tristar Division, attended one of the games at Southampton. The Hampshire officials made a big fuss of him and invited him to make the Man-of-the-Match presentation. It went down very well, so well that he offered me the job as National Sales Manager for Tristar – TNT's three-day delivery service – based in Atherstone.

I didn't want the job. I was happy and doing very well in Southampton. Gina was settled and we were on the verge of Scott coming into the world. I made the excuse that Gina was pregnant, about to give birth and she wouldn't move. That wasn't the end of it. He kept on at me throughout the summer, wanting me to take the job. I kept saying no. It reached mid-September and the phone rang. It was John Ovens. 'What are you earning at Southampton?'

'£20,000,' I said.

John came back with, 'I'll pay you £27,000, and there's a brand new, grey-coloured Audi 100 that comes with the job.' The significance of the colour of the car wasn't lost on me. Every other Audi 100 in the TNT UK fleet was red. This was too good to turn down.

'OK, I'll take it. When do I start?'

'But I thought you said you'd have trouble getting your wife to move.' I could detect a mixture of surprise and delight in his voice.

'Leave that with me. I'll sort things out at home. It'll be OK.'

I was to start immediately. The Tristar National Sales Conference was taking place at the Metropole Hotel in Birmingham on the Sunday, and they wanted me there on the Saturday for the rehearsal. I wasn't required to go on stage at such short notice, but my presence was required. Fair enough. The theme was 'out with the old & in with the new'. The 'old' was the outgoing National Sales Manager, Chris Atkinson. I was to be the 'new'. Chris was moving on to open a new division called AM Express. I was his replacement. Chris, or 'Atky' as he was known, was a pure salesman, something that I wasn't and would never be. He had worked his way up from being a Field Sales Executive at the Leicester depot.

Eventually he would be my right-hand man, in the same way I was The Jones' First Lieutenant. Had it not been for three leg breakages and a blood clot, Atky would have more than likely made the grade as a professional footballer. He'd been on Port Vale's books when a terrible catalogue of injuries curtailed his career. We shared a love of football. More pertinently, we had a common goal. We wanted to net sales and profits for TNT.

I drove up from Southampton, met and spoke with Chris. He said the job was pretty simple. I just needed to know if my daily consignment figures were up or down and why they were up or down. I'd be visiting the sales force around all the depots, motivating the people, ensuring the practices and procedures were being operated properly and the discount policy applied correctly.

Once I was in the conference hall I was asked, urged, cajoled – call it what you like – into addressing the 200 or so delegates the following day.

'You're here now. You've got to say something to the troops. It'll look a bit strange if you don't.' I walked on stage, took the microphone and mumbled something to the empty auditorium. It'd be a whole different ball game the following day.

My knees were knocking and my throat was as dry as the Gobi Desert on a particularly dry day. I was as nervous as hell. The last time I'd done any form of public speaking had been Huckleberry Finn & Tom Sawyer at Snodland Secondary School. I remembered Mr Bampton's advice: 'Speak to the last person at the very back of the room and everyone will hear you.' Tragically, Mr Bampton had died at a young age of a heart attack after I'd left the school. Years later it was his words which rang true and helped me through a nerve-wracking situation.

A couple of years later, I was having my annual appraisal with Bill Hanley, exploring my strengths and weaknesses. Bill said, 'So, what do you see as a weakness?'

I said, 'Public speaking.' Bill came straight back at me with his rich north-west twang, 'Well, you'd better get used to it because the way you're heading you'll be doing plenty of it.'

He was so right. I'd never lacked confidence, but addressing hundreds of people – with all eyes on me and everyone hanging on my every word – was a different kettle of fish. It wasn't going to be a weakness for much longer. I set my mind to it and became increasingly assured and accomplished. It reached a point where it didn't faze me at all. I could command an audience with ease, speak without notes in a coherent fashion for 20 minutes and deliver all of my key messages.

Three months after taking the job in Atherstone it was time to bring Gina and Scott up to their new home. On December 10th, 1984, I recalled the words I'd said to Tony Sim a few years prior: 'I'm not moving to the bloody Midlands.'

Well, here I was and I was most definitely moving to the bloody Midlands. The trip from Eastleigh to Warwickshire wasn't the best. There'd been a big smash on the M25 the day before in thick fog. It was national news. 24 hours later and the South East and the Midlands were still shrouded in the stuff.

Gina was nervous about the drive and had convinced herself our Vauxhall Viva wouldn't last the journey. I gave her the Audi 100 (in grey, so it blended in with the fog) and told her to follow me. The Viva wasn't a patch on the Audi, but Gina wasn't taking any chances.

She was determined to stay close, very bloody close, right up my arse in fact, on the A34! I kept waving at her to drop back. She just kept waving back at me. The message wasn't getting through. It all changed when a police car pulled her over on the outskirts of Oxford. It wasn't the thing to do, but I couldn't help myself. 'She's been tailgating me since Southampton, Officer,' I said, winding her up. The copper gave her a right bollocking, emphasising the correct braking distances, especially in light of the crash on the M25.

Gina wasn't happy, but I couldn't help laughing. If looks could've killed I'd have been a dead man. Drama over and Highway Code braking distances being observed, she followed me all the way to our new home, and the start of 35 years and counting, in Warwickshire. My job title said 'National Sales Manager' but I knew I wasn't a national sales manager. From day one I'd never really been comfortable in the role. I knew what I was – I was an operator, a general manager – I wasn't cut out for sales.

I'd done a budget review in early 1985 and, to be brutally honest, I hadn't made a very good job of it. It was the first time since I'd been with Inter County and now TNT that I'd experienced a hiccup in the upward trajectory of my career.

It was all about to change in a way I could never have envisaged in my wildest dreams. It began with a phone call on the night of Wednesday March 6th, 1985. I was hosting customers in the TNT corporate hospitality box at White Hart Lane, preparing to watch my beloved Spurs take on Real Madrid in the quarter final first leg of the UEFA Cup. It was a big match, one I'd been looking forward to for weeks, but I didn't see a single kick of the ball.

The crowd roared as battle between London's Lilywhites and Spain's Los Blancos commenced. It was billed as the main event, but the excitement didn't compare with how I was feeling at news of a top-secret project.

10

Bread and newspapers

'What do you know about papers?' It was a simple enough question.

'Well, I've a City and Guilds Certificate in paper-making, if that's any good, but apart from that not a lot,' was my somewhat naive and flippant reply.

Alan Jones was asking the question. My answer could've been so much better. Nonetheless, 'The Jones' came back with a surprising and unexpected endorsement. 'Good, I knew you were the man for me.' I hadn't a clue what he was on about.

Half an hour earlier, Alan had called Mike Rollo, Tottenham Hotspurs' Commercial Manager, and asked him to put me on the phone in the TNT corporate box at White Hart Lane. Mobile phones didn't exist in 1985.

'Tom, it's Alan. I need to see you. I'll be there in 30 minutes. Find somewhere private where we can talk.' I thought, *Oh Christ, what have I done?* Alan arrived just as the match kicked off. We made our way to the lounge reserved for box-holders. It was empty. Everyone who'd gone to White Hart Lane that night were there to watch Spurs and Real Madrid, me included – but something was happening, something significant – but what?

I sat down opposite Alan. The lounge was deserted but he still spoke in a hushed tone.

'You're not to breathe a word of this to anybody. I've just come from a meeting with Sir Peter, Ross Cribb and Rupert Murdoch. Murdoch wants us to get his papers out of two new printing works in Wapping and Glasgow. He says there'll be a lot of aggravation and strife with the print unions and it could get nasty.

'He wants us to put a proposal together to deliver his News International titles – *The Sun*, the *News Of The World*, *The Times* and *The Sunday Times*. The papers are to go to every retailer and newsagent in Britain – including Northern Ireland. It's a top-secret job and we'll only get one go at it. What do you think?'

What did I think? I thought it was one of the most exciting things I'd ever heard.

Sir Peter Abeles was the global Managing Director of TNT based in Australia. Ross Cribb was Sir Peter's right-hand man in his role as Director of Operations. Ross was affectionately known as 'The Coach', primarily for his love of Rugby League, but also for his superb motivational and man-management skills. The two men were the guiding force behind TNT's rise to prominence in the fast-moving, dog-eat-dog world of express parcels.

Sir Peter and Murdoch were mates, as well as business associates 'down under'. They shared a love of poker and would play as a two-man team. Can you imagine sitting down to face two of the sharpest business minds in Australia over a hand of poker? It must've been pretty daunting for any opponent, especially if the stakes were high. They were industrial heavyweights who placed great store on personal and professional integrity. Their word was their bond and a handshake on a deal was sacrosanct.

Murdoch was well aware of TNT's presence and pedigree in the UK. When he wanted to revolutionise the British newspaper business, he went on record as saying he would ask, '... my friends and partners in Australia, the TNT Transport Group...' to investigate the possibilities and practicalities of an independent distribution system for News International in Britain.

Alan said, 'We've a meeting lined up with Murdoch's consultant – Christopher Pole-Carew – tomorrow and I want you there representing TNT.'

As Managing Director of the publishers of the Nottingham Evening Post, Pole-Carew's claim to fame was that he'd confronted the unions during a six-week strike over the introduction of new technology. Three hundred printers lost their jobs and the unions lost all negotiating rights. It'd been enough to catch Murdoch's eye, and Pole-Carew was drafted in as a consultant at News International.

Right from the off I sussed that Pole-Carew was full of his own self importance. To say he was 'up himself' and somewhat eccentric was putting it mildly. He didn't appear to grasp the scale and magnitude of what lay ahead at Wapping and News International's other print plant, Kinning Park in Glasgow. His opening gambit was, 'You'll have to smear your bumpers with axle grease. It'll mean the pickets won't be able to get any grip on the vehicles when they try to overturn them.'

I soon put him right: 'Listen, we're talking about 32-ton trucks here, not bloody transit vans. There's no way pickets are overturning any TNT trucks.' Pole-Carew wasn't bringing anything of any worth to the party. We'd be doing this on our own – the TNT way – that's if we were doing it at all.

The next day I was summoned to a meeting at Claridge's Hotel in London. Those present would decide whether TNT would partner with Murdoch. A 'yes' vote could make his audacious bid to break the print union's stranglehold on the UK newspaper industry a reality. Murdoch, along with every other proprietor of the Fleet Street-based national press, had long been on the back foot, in the face of an overpaid, chronically over-manned workforce, hell-bent on using outmoded, laborious and inefficient equipment to justify their existence.

Restrictive practices, closed shops (only union members could be hired) and frequent wildcat strikes meant the unions were the tail wagging the dog. Murdoch had had enough of being held to ransom by the greedy, lazy and self-serving Society of Graphical & Allied Traders (SOGAT 82) and the more elitist National Graphical Association (NGA). The media mogul was going to blow decades of succumbing to outrageous practices and unreasonable union demands to smithereens. He needed TNT to help make it happen. His friend Sir Peter, who was staying at Claridge's, presided over the meeting, attended by Ross Cribb, Alan Jones, Bill Hanley, myself and Don Dick, a no-nonsense New Zealander and TNT's European supremo. I was asked the question, 'Should we, as a company, take the risk and all the accompanying flak and go for the News International contract?' I was 33 years old, ambitious and fearless. 'Of course we should do it. What an opportunity. How could we say no?' Bill Hanley quickly chipped in with a resounding 'yes'. The Jones was all for it. 'Yeah, yeah, yeah, I'm fully supportive.' Don Dick was a lone voice in rejecting the opportunity with an unequivocal 'no'. Don was adamant the risks were too high. The ramifications of taking on the unions could ruin the express parcels business. The knock-on effects would be terrible. TNT would be handing competitors the chance to capitalise on what would be a difficult and messy situation. Thankfully, Dick's lack of adventurism and negativity fell on deaf ears. He'd made the wrong call.

Sir Peter turned to Alan, Bill and myself. We were the ones who would be putting our backsides on the line if it all went wrong. 'How do you see the risks?' I fired straight back, before Alan or Bill could say a word. 'If we don't do it somebody else will. We can do it.' The decision was taken. We were indeed doing it.

I immediately moved out of my job as Tristar National Sales Manager. That was a big tick in the box from a personal perspective. I was back where I was destined to be – right in the thick of it.

I upped sticks from Express House and moved across Atherstone to a secret location. People were kept completely in the dark. Many thought I'd left the company overnight. One day there, the next day gone. To all intents and purposes, I and the small team entrusted with drawing up the News International proposal had dropped off the grid. Less than 72 hours after that initial call at Spurs, I was up and running. Along with two of Pole-Carew's men, Peter Crouch and John Hayden (both of whom were great guys who knew the newspaper industry and were nothing like their half barmy boss) we were assigned the title of Division 800. To the uninformed, 'Division 800' might sound like some mysterious covert operation, littered with intrigue. The reality was somewhat more mundane. It related to an accounting code, with all costs and expenses assigned to the News International proposal filed with an '800' prefix. It was a real adrenaline rush to have so much riding on the shoulders of so few. Time was of the essence and secrecy was paramount. Whatever else we did, we had to ensure that nobody – absolutely nobody – had so much of an inkling of what we were doing.

We had to ask questions, lots of questions. In my experience, if you're seen to be asking lots of questions, people begin to ask why. If we were to pull everything together for the News International proposal, we had to avoid arousing suspicion. We needed a viable cover story.

We came up with a 'half-baked' idea. It went down a treat.

Historically, News International, like all the national newspaper and magazine publishers, distributed their products via rail. The papers went to hundreds of wholesalers who, in turn, delivered to tens of thousands of newsagents and retailers. Murdoch's team had the data on the wholesalers but were clueless when it came to the identities and locations of the newsagents and shops. Those names and addresses sat with the wholesalers, and they weren't going to shoot themselves in the foot by giving us the list. We had to be cute. We had to be clever. We had to con our way into obtaining the information.

We went to see the National Federation of Newsagents. We told them TNT had been approached by a bakery company who wanted to deliver bread to newsagents throughout the country. They swallowed it and coughed up details on 26,000 retailers. It'd worked like a dream, but our intelligence suggested there were nearer to 50,000 outlets where Murdoch's papers were sold on a daily basis. A lot more digging would be required on that front.

News International provided us with their production schedules. From these I had to work out the levels of equipment and manpower required and, most crucial of all, the timeframes to ensure the papers reached their destinations to optimise sales. Newspapers are one of the most perishable products on the planet. If you don't get them out on time they're of little use to anybody, unless you're using them as fish and chip wrappings.

The fictitious bakery cover story was maintained as more and more people were brought into the loop. TNT's purchasing and engineering departments began to get involved. It was critical that nothing leaked out about our real intentions.

The operational proposal was ready on April 16th, 1985 – barely a month since the initial approach to TNT. We'd done our homework and were ready to show how we'd help make Wapping and Kinning Park a success. That said, when I received the call telling me we were meeting Murdoch, it wasn't the best of timing.

I'd just arrived in Derbyshire for a caravanning weekend with Gina and Scott. We'd set up on the Friday evening, when Alan phoned the site and told me I was needed down in London for an 11am start. We were sitting down with Murdoch at his apartment in St James's Place.

I won't lie, it was an exciting prospect, one which was further heightened when I was given the seat immediately to the left of Murdoch in the meeting. I was sitting next to one of the world's most powerful media and business moguls. I felt more alive than I'd ever been in my life. It felt good – really good. Alan and Bill sat to the left of me.

Murdoch's team included Bruce Matthews, Managing Director

of News International, Bill Gillespie, Managing Director of Times Newspapers, Charlie Wilson, Editor of The Times and Ken Taylor, Technical Director of News Group Newspapers. Taylor was the 'architect' of the Wapping plant. He knew every building, every screw, every rafter of what was later to become Fortress Wapping. I remember glancing at a sheet of A4 paper Murdoch had in front of him. It was his agenda for the day. It read:

- Meet TNT
- Lunch
- Heathrow Airport – take Concorde to New York
- Take children out to dinner
- JFK Airport – take British Airways back to London

He took the piece of paper and tore it into four equal squares. As the meeting progressed he jotted numbers down on each square – no text, just figures. By the time he was ready to populate the fourth square he turned to me and said, 'Right, Tom, take me through it.' I gave him an overview of the proposal and he wrote a few more digits on the previously empty fourth square. He seemed to like what I'd said. Then the number crunching began.

Murdoch, in typical forthright fashion, said, 'How much is this going to cost me?'

Alan responded, 'We don't know at this stage, it hasn't been fully costed – this is just an initial proposal.'

Murdoch looked at me. 'How many of these tractor units will you need?'

'Approximately 34, plus an extra 30 at weekends,' I said.

'How many trailers?'

'About 90, with an extra three at weekends,' I replied.

'How many vans?'

'I'd imagine something in the region of 780, with an additional four rigid vehicles during the week and one extra at weekends,' I responded.

Murdoch continued in the same vein, 'Let's start with the tractor units. How much are they each?' Alan answered, 'We'll have to talk to the suppliers. We'd only be guessing at this stage.'

Murdoch: 'Tom, how much are they?'

'£30,000 each,' I said.

Murdoch: 'Trailers – how much are they a-piece?'

Alan: 'We don't know, we'd have to get on to the suppliers.'

Murdoch: 'Tom, how much are they?'

'Between £20,000 and £25,000 each.'

Murdoch: 'These vans – how much will they cost?'

Alan: 'We couldn't say for sure, we'd have to get a quote off the suppliers.'

Murdoch: 'Tom, how much are they?'

'About £18,000 each.'

Murdoch: 'How much will you pay the drivers?'

Alan: 'We'd have to negotiate with the union.'

Murdoch: 'How much, Tom?'

'About £500 each route.'

Within minutes Murdoch declared, 'You're going to be charging me £1 million per week.'

Alan: 'We don't know at the moment.'

Murdoch: 'Tom, how much?'

'We'll go away and work it all out and get back to you.'

Murdoch hadn't disappointed. He was impressive. It wasn't difficult to see why he was where he was in the world. Astute and with a speed of thought that was astonishing, I was staggered how he'd simply written down the key numbers, without any worded reference points, and calculated all the figures.

The meeting concluded at around 3pm. Alan, Bill and I drove straight back to Atherstone. We had people getting prices for this, prices for that. What was the availability? How soon could we have them? What discount would we get if we bought a certain number? The pace was frenetic. To those who weren't in the know, it must've looked like an extraordinary effort to deliver some bread.

After non-stop working we arrived at a figure late on the Sunday night. TNT would be charging Rupert Murdoch £1,067,000 per week to get his newspapers out of Wapping and Kinning Park. It had taken TNT – as a company – 30 hours to arrive at the quote. Rupert Murdoch had, near as dammit, done the same in less than 15 minutes.

I remember running off 12 copies of the fully-costed proposal at four o'clock on the Monday morning. They were to be the only copies in existence. I've kept copy number six to this day. I regard it as something of a personal treasure – one of my finest achievements.

Murdoch liked what he saw and accepted the deal. It was revised at a later date when News International, quite unexpectedly, came to an agreement with all the wholesalers outside of London. TNT's new brief would see us deliver to wholesalers in the provinces but not in the capital. When it came to London we had the task of getting the papers to every newsagent and retailer, and there were thousands of them! We undertook hundreds of nocturnal reconnaissance missions to locate each and every one.

Operating under cover of darkness, the aim was not to attract attention. In some instances it had the polar opposite effect. Our 'scouts' were getting arrested for 'kerb crawling', with 'concerned' residents and members of the public reporting 'suspicious-looking vehicles' idling and loitering in streets and neighbourhoods. All our people stuck with the bakery story, even when being questioned by the police. We would be delivering bread in the middle of the night, so it made perfect sense to go on dummy runs in the small hours.

The revised proposal would cost Murdoch around £500,000 per week, with News International also underwriting TNT for any medical bills if our people were attacked and injured, as well as damage to any vehicles or any TNT assets such as depots or offices.

The bespoke nature of the contract called for specially designed trailers, complete with canopies on both sides. This would enable us to operate in all weathers when offloading the papers to up to eight vans at any time. Murdoch gave us the green light to order all the equipment specified in the proposal. I attended the Commercial Motor Show at Birmingham's National Exhibition Centre in 1985. Volkswagon and Scania must've thought Christmas had come early. I placed orders for 780 VW LT45 vans and 34 Scania tractor units. That summer, Volkswagon kept an entire production line going in Germany during their annual two-week shutdown, to ensure they could meet our order. For the 40-foot trailers, I went to our usual suppliers – Cartwrights of Accrington in Lancashire – only this time with a modified brief. I wanted all the trailers to have the floors sloping slightly inwards from each side. This meant the bundles of papers could be loaded individually, with little or no chance of them falling off the wagon. It was a small detail, but it would make life a damn sight easier when Wapping went into production mode. All three of our suppliers delivered on time. We had the machinery sorted. I now had to make sure we'd have the right people on the job.

I instructed all the depot managers to compile lists of what I called 'suitable' drivers. I needed bona fide drivers who'd be loyal to the company and wouldn't be intimidated if it all kicked off. I didn't want diehard union militants or extreme left-wingers driving our wagons. We'd have enough trouble with violent picket lines. We needed to avoid shitting on our own doorstep. The drivers on the lists were all vetted and security-checked by external consultants. The process would serve us well throughout the war of attrition with the unions – with one notable exception – one that would later make national newspaper headlines.

We were as prepared as we would ever be and ready to go.

In the days, weeks and months following my conversation with Alan Jones at White Hart Lane, I'd made it my business to learn all I could about News International and Fleet Street in general.

Bill Gillespie, the MD of *The Times* – an Irishman and a lovely fella – gave Bill Handley and me a tour of *The Times*' building in Farringdon Road. To say it was an eye-opener would be a massive understatement. He shared some of his frustrations, explaining what the printers would do to disrupt production, and how they basically just took the piss. He led us to what used to be the Hot Metal Room. It had long since been rendered redundant, apart from one activity – one which I could hardly believe. It was approaching half past ten on this particular night when Bill opened the door. There before us, as brazen as you like, were SOGAT 82 and NGA members getting into sleeping bags and going to sleep for the night – a night that they would be paid, for doing absolutely sweet fuck all.

'Goodnight, Bill,' said one. 'Night, Mr Gillespie,' said another. I was gobsmacked. We came away from the room.

'What's that all about?' I asked. 'What the fuck are they doing? Aren't they supposed to be working?' I'd have sacked them there and then. Billy could see my anger and incredulity.

'I'd love to, Tom, but if I did, all the other buggers would down tools and walk out and we'd lose the edition. There'd be a strike and we'd lose a lot more than we'd gain,' he said with a weary air of resignation. The strength of the unions was plain to see. It was hideous.

Bill told us about an occasion when *The Sunday Times* magazine was a week late being published. Everything had been agreed on the Saturday, the pagination and the editorial content, but at the last minute the Picture Editor wanted to change the image on the front cover. It was quite straightforward – simply swap one picture for another. The print unions refused to handle the magazine. It didn't go out. A week later, following negotiations with the union and more money being paid to SOGAT 82 and NGA members, the magazine was published. It was yet another illustration of the sheer unadulterated bloody madness that was accepted as normal practice.

Bill gave us another example of the print union's blatant dishonesty. The fire alarm went off at *The Sun* and *News Of The World*'s printing press in Bouverie Street. 220 print workers had signed in for the night shift. When the roll call number was counted there were only 140 present. The other 80 were either in the pub or at home in bed. They weren't required, because it didn't take 220 men to do the job in hand. It only needed 140, but the unions demanded the extra 80 men clock on and basically commit fraud with impunity.

It was the union shop stewards, known as the Fathers of The Chapel, who determined how many men were needed on a print run – clearly 220 was way over the top. The union knew it, News International knew it, but at that time Murdoch would have had a full-blown strike on his hands if he'd have taken action.

SOGAT 82 and the NGA were also crafty buggers. Their members would be spread around the different national papers – *The Sun*, *Daily Mirror*, *Daily Express*, *Daily Mail*, *The Guardian*, *Daily Telegraph*, *The Times* – working so many nights of the week on one title and so many on others. It meant if there was a strike at *The Sun*, a printer could still have a wage coming in from the *Mirror*, the *Mail* or the *Express* or wherever. Whichever way you cut it, the print worker's best interests would always be served.

The TNT proposal would also help eliminate other ludicrous work practices, one example being the unneccessary time-consuming and costly activities of labelling newspaper bundles.

One of the first things I said when Murdoch asked me to walk him through TNT's proposal was, 'I don't need the bundles labelled. At any one time I'll be carrying two products – *The Sun* and *The Times* during the week, and the *News Of The World* and *The Sunday Times* on a Saturday night. They're very distinct from each other. All I need to know is how many bundles I'll be carrying and how many 'turns' there are in each bundle.' Murdoch's men seemed surprised at my suggestion. I heard murmurings of disquiet. Rupert showed no reaction. The papers had always been labelled.

Like so many elements of the pre-Wapping era, it was about to be killed off.

A bundle was a stack of newspapers. The 'turn' was where the papers were turned in alternating directions to assist in counting the number of papers in a bundle. For example, if we were handling a bundle of 200 copies of *The Sun*, there could be eight turns of 25 papers each. It made the process of counting and delivering the right amount of papers, particularly to the retailers, faster and more efficient.

One of the most bizarre things I came across on my 'research' at News International occurred on a visit to Kinning Park. In the days of hot metal printing, the newspaper companies employed 'Blessers', men who would manually tie up and label the bundles of papers. The action of placing the labels on the bundles – similar to that of a clergyman placing his hand on a churchgoer and giving them God's blessing – earned them their job title.

Inside the Glasgow print plant were a series of conveyor belts to carry the papers from the presses out to the delivery vans. There'd be a 10-metre-long conveyor and then a metre gap before another 10-metre length of conveyor. It didn't make sense. Why wasn't the conveyor belt joined up?

'Oh, that's so the Blesser can pass them from one conveyor belt to the other,' came the answer. It was another outrageous example of the power of the print unions. An utterly meaningless role still existed in the industry because it suited the unions. I don't know what it cost Murdoch to move to Wapping, but he must've saved a bloody fortune on ridding himself of chronic over-manning. The 670 printers employed at Wapping would produce the same number of papers as the 6,800 men previously employed at the Grays Inn Road and Bouverie Street print plants. Now, that's efficiency.

Another Spanish practice was doubling and sometimes trebling up on delivery drivers. Whenever the papers were driven to a London railhead, the unions would insist on having two of their members in the cab. If they were going outside of the M25, it required three – God knows why. On one occasion a News International lorry came off the road on the way down to Southampton. Police found two of the 'drivers' shaken but uninjured in a field. The 'third man' was nowhere to be found. Just like the fire alarm roll call at Bouverie Street, the union member was at home in bed.

No wonder Rupert Murdoch was determined to rid himself of such anarchic practices.

Throughout the contract negotiations with TNT, Murdoch had always insisted he would give us between six and eight weeks' notice before Wapping and Kinning Park went live. For some reason, I always doubted it. I could never see it happening that way. Thankfully I had the nous to put management teams and structures in place throughout the TNT network, thereby massively enhancing our levels of preparedness. Murdoch had agreed to the additional costs – it was as if we were both on the same wavelength and knew what was coming.

On Friday January 24th, 1986, eight weeks' notice suddenly shrank to 24 hours. The newly acquired and rapidly assembled TNT Newsfast fleet was mobilised. Murdoch was through with talking to the unions. On Saturday 25th January, 1986, he pushed the button, started the Wapping presses running on the *News Of The World* and *The Sunday Times* and ushered in a new era for the UK newspaper industry. It was the beginning of the end of union mob rule. It was time for our wagons – *my wagons* – to roll.

11

Murdoch and Wapping

I went to work on a cold day in the winter of 1986. I had every expectation of being at home with Gina and Scott that same evening. It didn't happen. I was meeting with Rupert Murdoch in London. I had no idea that it'd be early March before I'd next sleep in my own bed in my house in Warwickshire.

On that particular day, Friday, January 24th, 6,000 union members employed by News International went on strike. Murdoch sacked the lot. Exhaustive negotiations had failed to reach agreement on Murdoch's plans to switch to new printing technology. It was a move that would strip the unions of the power they had wielded and abused for countless years.

A bitter and often violent 54-week industrial dispute was about to commence. To call it a dispute doesn't do it justice. There were times when I witnessed sights more akin to a war zone. By the time the 'Wapping Dispute' finally petered out on February 5th, 1987, there'd been 1,500 arrests, 574 Metropolitan Police officers injured, along with dozens of TNT drivers and 'members of the public', plus 1,200 attacks on TNT Newsfast vehicles and premises.

It didn't match up to the hatred and social divisions exposed by the miners' strike of 1984-85, but by the time it was over Prime

Minister Margaret Thatcher would have achieved her second major victory over the trade union movement.

Wapping undoubtedly had political similarities with the miners' dispute – it was motivated by a far left agenda and involved thousands of people who had no direct link with the employment issues at hand. They were rent-a-mob militants and anarchists who were up for a scrap.

SOGAT 82 and the NGA called for a union-wide boycott of all Murdoch's papers. They were relying on their 'brothers and sisters' in the rail unions to ensure they weren't distributed. This, they assumed, would bring News International back to the negotiating table. They hadn't banked on TNT. We were Murdoch's trump card. We would provide a direct door-to-door delivery service that was faster, more reliable and less expensive than the existing British Rail system. We would be instrumental in enabling Murdoch to bring the print unions to their knees.

By 3pm on Saturday January 25th, 1986, a fleet of TNT wagons was inside the fortified Wapping plant, surrounded by nine-foot-high palisade fencing and row upon row of razor wire. The pickets were bristling with violent intent, howling derision at what they saw as the betrayal by our drivers – the Judases of the TGWU – who'd breached the sanctity of an official union picket line. They were putting down a marker for what lay ahead for the rest of that year.

Instead of the familiar orange and white TNT livery, our vehicles were white tractor units and blue curtain-sided 40-foot-long trailers. The pickets called them the 'Blue Rats'. We didn't want to advertise who we were to the mob and the wider trade union movement, but it didn't make any difference. By Sunday morning, everybody knew it was TNT working for Murdoch.

It was a momentous day for Murdoch, but his body language belied the fact he had so much riding on the success of this daring departure from Fleet Street. He was calm and composed as he surveyed the line of trucks. 'You've done the easy bit, you've got them in. Can you get them back out again?' If ever there was a $64,000 question, that was it.

The print presses were due to start rolling at 6pm. They didn't. Neither were they producing by 7pm or 8pm. Technical problems were delaying the dawn of a new age of national UK newspaper production. As the clock ticked on and there was still no signs of any papers being produced, I went up to Murdoch. 'Rupert, my drivers are running out of hours. We're already cutting it fine to get to some of the far-flung areas. If the presses aren't rolling soon we've no chance of hitting Wales, Norfolk or the West Country.' I suggested something which wasn't entirely logical but would be hugely symbolic.

'Let's send the lorries out empty.' Murdoch agreed. We would send two wagons to Devon and Cornwall and two to West Wales. There wouldn't be any papers on them, but the pickets and the unions would be none the wiser. As the minutes passed by it was 8.45pm. The presses were still silent. The picket line was anything but. The rabble-rousing chants and insults were carrying through the crisp night air. The mob was oblivious to what was about to happen.

As I stood on the ramp outside I heard them start up. Four Scania tractor units revved into life, pulled out of the loading hall and gathered speed crossing the compound. As they hit fourth gear the gates swung open and out they went. The juggernauts scythed through the seething mass of protestors and out into the night. Yes, they were empty, but it didn't matter. We'd got them in and we'd got them out. I knew at that moment we'd cracked it.

No matter what was to come, we'd established we could get in and out of Wapping and we'd get the job done for News International. Murdoch recognised it as well. A palpable sense of relief flooded my senses, and yet not a single paper had been printed, let alone gone through the gates. The union's last hope was a call to TNT's drivers – the majority of whom were members of the Transport & General Workers Union – to stop crossing the picket lines at Wapping. TGWU General Secretary, Ron Todd, and his Deputy Bill Morris pleaded with our drivers to show solidarity. Their appeals fell on deaf ears.

Over a year later, when the dispute had ended, SOGAT's General Secretary, Brenda Dean, admitted she knew they'd lost the strike the day the first lorry came down the ramp and out of Wapping. At least we agreed on something. I'd said exactly the same on that Saturday night.

By 9pm I had drivers who were out of hours and could not legally drive. It was a bit different back in my day as a knight of the road, but I digress. I went to Murdoch, 'I've got drivers completely out of hours. They can't go anywhere tonight.'

Murdoch asked, 'How many?' 'About a dozen,' I said.

'Check them all into the Tower Hotel. I'll pay. I'll come down with you.' It was one thing Murdoch footing the bill for the drivers, but quite another that he took time out to accompany the drivers to the snazzy 5-star hotel. Rupert had a couple of the drivers with him in his chauffeur-driven car, I had three or four in my car, with the rest in two vehicles in a mini-convoy, complete with a police escort. It was literally a five-minute run from Wapping to the hotel, but Murdoch's gesture would resonate forever and a day with those TNT drivers. They couldn't believe that Rupert Murdoch was taking the time to check them in at reception on one of the most important nights of his life.

'Everything and anything you want tonight is on me, and I do mean everything,' Rupert told the drivers. It was a PR masterstroke by Murdoch. The drivers were already committed to their jobs and getting News International's papers out of the plant and past the pickets, but this would take their loyalty to a whole new level. It went down a storm with all of the other drivers when their colleagues told them what Murdoch had done.

Murdoch and I returned to the plant. The presses finally rolled into action. They were still printing at 10am on Sunday. The delays meant the print runs were down in numbers. We couldn't deliver what we didn't have, but there were still hundreds of thousands of editions printed and ready for distribution. As the bundles began accumulating I turned to one of the News International Circulation directors. 'Where are the loaders?'

'What do you mean, loaders?' came the perplexed response.

I said, 'Well, who's going to load the bundles of papers onto the trailers?'

'Well, you are – TNT,' said the director in an indignant tone.

'We haven't been asked to quote for it; it's not us,' I said. Christ, they haven't any fucking loaders! What a cock-up. They dragged these guys out of the offices, the computer rooms, anywhere they could find them, to load the trailers. The next day the poor buggers could hardly walk. They obviously weren't used to manual labour.

Great swathes of the country didn't get any News International papers on the Sunday, but we got them into London. The fact there was a visible presence of the *NOTW* and *The Sunday Times* on the streets of the capital was a moral victory.

Later that night, *The Sun* and *The Times* were due to print for the first time at Wapping. Once again, Murdoch was beset by production problems. The guys doing the printing weren't printers, they were electricians, and they were in unchartered territory.

The hiccup with the loaders was addressed with an agency bussing people in from Milton Keynes. On Monday 27th January, 1986, the first Wapping produced and printed edition of *The Sun* hit the streets under the headline, **'A NEW SUN IS RISING TODAY'**. It was a fresh start for *The Sun*, but I was feeling far from fresh. I was knackered. I hadn't been to bed since the Thursday night. Murdoch had given us the green light on the Friday morning and it'd been a 72-hour whirlwind, the like of which I'd never before experienced in my life. I'd been running on adrenaline for three days and nights. I was shattered.

For the next six weeks I fell into a gruelling daily work pattern where I'd spend up to 18 hours a day inside Fortress Wapping, slipping back to the Tower Hotel to snatch a few hours' sleep, a shower and a full English breakfast. I was doing well if I managed four hours' sleep in any 24-hour period. It was incredibly demanding. It didn't go unnoticed. I was in the plant one day, and Murdoch and John Cowley, the Joint General Manager of News International, were walking towards me down the corridor. I heard Murdoch say, '*Here he comes, the man who never sleeps.*' It was both a statement of fact and a compliment. Looking back, I don't know how I managed to do it, but I was young, I was determined and I was dedicated, but boy, it was tough going.

The first few weeks were plagued with production problems and extreme picketing. The mob was feral. At least half a dozen windscreens were being smashed every night, as rocks and bricks rained down on our vehicles.

The picket numbers were swelled as militant lefties came in by the coach load from Cannock, Leicester, Nottingham and Wales. They weren't print workers, they just wanted to cause violence and wreak havoc with the police. It was mayhem, with Wednesday and Saturday nights the worst, Saturday being the worst of the worst.

The police would create diversions and give protection to convoys of up to half a dozen TNT vehicles at a time, along with several cars carrying journalists, as they made a dash through the gates. Threats, intimidation and violence were the norm. News International workers would be followed home and their property and cars would be damaged. The one good thing about my exile in London was Gina and Scott were up in the Midlands, out of harm's way.

Five weeks into the job and I hit rock bottom. I hadn't been home. The production problems seemed endless. We couldn't deliver on time because the bloody print runs were never on time. Like everybody else, I had the 'Wapping Cough', a horrible tickly throat caused by exhaust fumes in the loading hall. The area was never designed to take 40ft articulated lorries. The extractor fans just couldn't cope. I was outside standing on the ramp. It was what we'd call a 'dank' night in Scotland – a light drizzle that goes through you. Cold and wet, suffering from severe sleep deprivation, I was ready to jack it in. I was in tears, literally crying. I was thinking, *Fuck it, let somebody else take over.* That night the presses suddenly kicked in properly. The production ran on time and we delivered on time. The schedules that I'd painstakingly researched and drafted for the TNT proposal document were suddenly happening for the first time. At the very point I was ready to quit, everything came good. It was my Eureka moment. The gods had finally deigned to smile on me.

The scale of the job had to be seen to be believed. It was astonishing, more so because it was groundbreaking. Each week we were delivering newspapers weighing 5.4 million tonnes, comprising:

- 27,000,000 copies of *The Sun*
- 3,300,000 copies of *The Times*
- 5,100,000 copies of the *News Of The World*
- 1,425,000 copies of *The Sunday Times*

We were reaching well over a thousand wholesalers and 4,500 newsagents and retailers. It was a complex operation, one which required courage, endurance, innovation, expertise and flexibility. Whatever plaudits we earned were well deserved.

Throughout the dispute we'd have regular weekly briefings with the Metropolitan Police. Commander Wyn Jones was in overall charge of operations. Jones was widely regarded as a future potential Commissioner. He rose to the rank of Assistant Commissioner before his career later ended in disgrace, amid misconduct charges and a criminal conviction for shoplifting.

On one particular occasion the police asked that we call all the drivers together in the canteen for a special briefing at 3pm on a Saturday. They wanted to implement a new colour-coded system of routes out of the plant to catch the pickets off-guard. The police gave a big-screen presentation of three different exit routes – one in red, one in blue and one in green. Meticulous planning had gone into it and the police would clear the chosen route on the night, calling the 'colour' seconds before the trucks departed.

Each driver was handed an information pack. The system would go live later that evening. Of course, drivers being drivers (trust me, I was once one of them), they left the briefing, threw the packs to one side and went off for a cup of tea, a bite to eat or even a sleep before that night's run. We had eight 40ft wagons ready to go and the police called the signal, 'RED ROUTE'. The drivers pulled the maps out of their packs, only to find the coppers had photo-copied all the routes in black and white! It didn't matter if it was red, blue or green, everything was grey. Chaos ensued, with vehicles going all different ways trying to remember which one was red. Needless to say, the plan was scrapped that night.

The drivers, who'd been so carefully selected and vetted for security purposes, were doing everybody proud. They were coping with extreme acts of violence. A rock was thrown off a bridge in London, straight through a windscreen of a TNT vehicle travelling at 40mph. It attracted TV news coverage. When the reporter asked me if these attacks would intimidate the drivers, I was able to give a strong and truthful riposte, 'No, it won't. If anything, it'll make them more determined to get through. We've a job to do and we're doing it!'

Another story which hit the headlines related to the one and only example where our security vetting slipped up.

A union infiltrator managed to go under the radar when the driver lists were compiled. He was an ex-Luton Town councillor. He'd been forced to resign for giving priority to women on council house waiting lists in return for sex. The little weasel had also lied on his TNT application form. He somehow sustained injuries on the job. One theory was that he'd slipped in the depot and banged his head on a coffee machine. Another was that his colleagues had discovered he was a union snitch and given him a good hiding.

Either way, nothing could be proven. The left-wing press, such as the *Daily Mirror* and the communist rag, *The Morning*

Star, ran stories praising this 'worthy driver' who'd been assaulted by Murdoch-supporting bullies. The *News Of The World* took a different stance with a headline, 'YOU LYING TRUCKER'. It's now 33 years on, and I still smile at that piece of journalistic wit. The one bad apple aside, the rest of the drivers were superb.

Despite the daily threats, the provocation from pickets and the risk of being hurt, they were incredibly resilient. When I said the attacks on vehicles would only make them more determined I wasn't peddling propaganda, it was absolutely true. They were a remarkable bunch who had a devilish sense of humour. I walked into the canteen one Saturday afternoon when they were running a sweepstake. The winner would be the driver who succeeded in taking down blue balloons tied to the union's makeshift support vehicle – a double-decker bus parked behind the picket line in Wellclose Square.

The irony of the bus was that it had parked directly above a manhole cover, beneath which ran all the power lines into Wapping. The protestors could've caused real disruption if they'd damaged the cables, but they were blissfully ignorant and ill informed. They were the same on most matters throughout the entire 54 weeks.

At the height of the dispute, the then TNT UK Chairman, Peter Allsebrook, came to visit the plant as a morale booster – not that the drivers needed their morale boosting. They were all lined up on the ramp as a show of respect for the chairman's flying visit. Peter – who was a lovely chap, proper gentleman and a Second World War hero – addressed the men.

'I've just come from the Prime Minister at Number 10 Downing Street, and she wants me to tell you you're all doing a wonderful job.' He didn't get the response he expected.

'Big Pat', a driver from Leicester who'd had his windscreen put through on most Wednesday and Saturday nights, said, 'Well, tell her to show her appreciation in the fucking wage packet!'

Surprised and somewhat taken aback, Peter turned to me and said, 'Is he joking?'

I couldn't help but grin, 'No, he's deadly serious.'

Driver safety was one of my main concerns as they drove through the gates, but the Wapping plant itself was one of the most secure places I've ever known. For all the threats, protests and violence, the pickets never had a cat in hell's chance of getting in. I was key to the success of the operation, but even I had limited access within the building. It was on the first anniversary – January 25th, 1987 – that Murdoch's Security Director, Stuart Edwards, took me to a bunker that I didn't know existed. It had banks of screens displaying all the approach roads and side streets around the site, all the corridors inside the building and all the outside areas within the compound. The piece de resistance were the screens showing infrared images of all the picket lines. News International had been monitoring everything that had gone on under cover of darkness, via strategically placed infrared cameras. It was very impressive. It would've been even more so, had we – TNT – been aware of them the previous year. Despite the lack of transparency between the News International security team and ourselves, we'd still got through every single night.

TNT depots didn't have the benefit of such advanced security systems and some were attacked by militants. Three vehicles were burned out at my old stomping ground in Southampton. The old Inter County Express headquarters at Ramsbottom depot suffered damage, but the most 'spectacular' attack occurred at Thetford in Norfolk, when flares and rockets landed on the depot.

As the first anniversary approached, the dispute was all but over. Brenda Dean had known she was fighting a losing battle from day one. The print unions had been stripped of their industrial clout, but Murdoch and his management team, along with Commander Jones and the Met, suspected the militants wanted one last hurrah, one last 'excuse' to vent their wrath on Wapping.

They were right. At the police briefing on Friday 23rd January, 1987, Jones declared that he was, 'Going after the troublemakers.' The next night was violent – extremely violent. It was as bad as it had ever been the year before – a time when the unions were still deluded enough to think they could beat Murdoch. The pickets were pushing gas bottles down the hill, trying to ignite them as they rolled towards the gates. Flares and fireworks were going off. I saw what must have been a couple of thousand rioters pulling at the palisade fencing. I swear I saw it move and bend, but it stayed intact.

But, irony of ironies, we had a trouble free night. The pickets and the police were so busy fighting each other nobody paid any attention to the trucks. We just drove in and out as we pleased. We didn't need pre-arranged convoys. It was bizarre. In early February the dispute officially ended. Life at Wapping became something of an anti-climax. I'd grown used to the picketing and commotion. Suddenly, it'd all gone. It was a different world.

Similarly, the meeting at Claridge's, when TNT had agreed to take on the News International contract, seemed an age ago. Don Dick had been vehemently opposed to the idea, whereas Bill Hanley had been 100% behind it. In the course of the endless days I spent at Wapping, I have vivid memories of two phone calls, one from Don, the other from Bill.

Don was totally against the job. He'd never set foot inside Wapping or been anywhere near the place. He called me on a Sunday morning at the Tower Hotel. I'd returned from yet another demanding Saturday night, albeit the operation was now running smoothly.

The phone rang bang on eight o'clock. 'Tom. It's Don. Call me back at 8.20.'

'Yes, certainly, Mr Dick.' I replaced the receiver. It came to 8.20 and I thought I'd give him a couple of extra minutes or so. I rang back at 8.25.

'When I fucking tell you to ring me back at twenty past, I mean twenty past!' came the bollocking down the phone.

'Oh, sorry, Mr Dick.' I hadn't expected that!

The tone in Don's voice changed, 'Well, I just wanted you to know we think you're doing a brilliant job and we're very proud of you.'

You could've knocked me down with a feather, 'Oh, err, well, thank you, Don, that's really appreciated.' The line went dead. It was the one and only time I ever received any recognition from him over Wapping. I always had tremendous admiration and respect for the TNT hierarchy – Sir Peter, Ross Cribb, The Jones and Bill Hanley – but Don Dick was the exception. He was obnoxious. It's one thing being 'businesslike' without any niceties, but Don seemed incapable of actually being pleasant. His man management skills were non-existent.

He'd originally brokered the deal to acquire Inter County Express at Sir Peter Abeles' behest, and he obviously knew the parcels business inside and out, but he'd completely misread the deal with News International. I've often wondered if our success rankled with him. He certainly could never bask in any reflected glory.

It wouldn't surprise me if he was told to make that call. It wasn't in his nature to be fulsome with any praise – certainly not to someone who'd proven him wrong.

The second call that I'll always remember came from Bill Hanley on New Year's Eve 1986. I was working in the plant as per usual. It was the night of the TNT Christmas and New Year party. It was always held at The Swan Hotel in Harrogate, and it was a bloody good 'do', with partners, a good band, excellent food and great company.

The phone rang in my office – a less than luxurious portacabin.

'How's it going, lad?' I recognised the voice immediately.

'It's alright, Bill. We're on time. We're doing OK.' I asked how the 'do' was going.

'Good, as usual, bloody good. The reason I'm calling is to tell you we've just had a toast to 'Absent friends'.'

'Absent friends?' I queried. 'What do you mean, absent friends?'

'Your tables are set – those of you at Wapping and Kinning Park – your tables are all set, but of course they're empty because you're working. I'm just calling to let you know that we've all toasted you in your absence,' said Bill. It was a simple and thoughtful gesture. I found it very touching and really appreciated the call.

It'd been such a demanding year, but also rewarding on many different levels. We'd secured and delivered on a very profitable contract with News International – a deal which would soon open up a myriad of other opportunities. My profile and stock had rocketed within TNT and would help me rise through the ranks and, on a more personal level, it'd been fascinating working alongside Rupert Murdoch.

He divided opinion back in the 80s – even more so today – but I could not help but admire the guy. He was a visionary who strode forward and let others follow. He also led by example and didn't suffer fools gladly.

I remember him coming into Wapping in the early hours of the morning with his then wife, Anna, to see if the printing was running to schedule. He was casually dressed in a pair of trainers, slacks, shirt and a yellow cashmere jumper. I was in the tote room where the presses could be monitored via a system of colour-coded bars on a bank of computer screens. A red bar meant the press wasn't printing. A yellow bar showed the press was producing unusable, poor quality printing. A white bar indicated good quality printing. John Cowley came in and told Murdoch, 'We're going to lose D4,' and proceeded to go into technical detail as to what was wrong with that particular press.

Murdoch listened and then left the room. He returned 30 minutes later, his beautiful yellow cashmere jumper covered in grease. He told Cowley to watch the screen, which showed a red bar – D4 wasn't working. It quickly went from red to yellow to white. The press was now fully operational. Murdoch turned to Cowley and, in a withering tone, said, 'Don't you ever tell me you've lost a press again.' Point made. The proprietor of the paper, the top man, wasn't afraid to get his hands dirty and show his people how it should be done.

My abiding memory is one of Murdoch's lovely yellow cashmere jumper, smeared in oil and completely ruined. I vowed that one day I'd be the proud owner of a cashmere jumper. Six months later, I was in Harrods and treated myself to a cashmere jumper. It was yellow.

On another occasion, some Scottish football results led to an interesting exchange with Murdoch. I was always at Wapping on the Saturday afternoon, and as soon as the first papers came off the press I'd be looking for the football results. On this particular day I noticed all the games in the Scottish Second Division had finished 0-0, every game. I knew that couldn't be right. I went up to one of Murdoch's Circulation Directors. 'You've got a problem here.'

He said, 'What do you mean?'

I said, 'All the Scottish Second Division results are saying 0-0. There's no way that's right. Something's gone wrong somewhere.'

'No, no,' said Murdoch's man in a dismissive tone, 'They'll be right.'

A quarter of a million copies of the *NOTW* later and the penny dropped. They hadn't all been scoreless draws. Murdoch saw me the next day. 'What happened, Tom?' I told him I'd reported it to the Circulation Director, but he'd insisted the games had all ended goalless. I don't know about goalless, I just thought the bloke was bloody gormless.

I said, 'To tell you the truth, Rupert, I wouldn't give him a job in a TNT Traffic Office.' Murdoch frowned, nodded his head and walked away.

Later in the day he came up to me. 'That fella you said you wouldn't employ in a TNT Traffic Office,' he paused for a second. 'You won't be seeing him around here anymore.'

I didn't like to ask if he'd been sacked or just moved out of Wapping, but it demonstrated that, if you weren't up to the job, under Murdoch you were gone.

I'd describe Murdoch as a 'typical Aussie', a go-getter with a real lust for life. He wasn't afraid to take risks, but they were finely calculated and he reaped the rewards. The new technology facilitated bigger newspapers. His News International titles were now free of historical limitations on the number of pages. Increased pagination equalled more space for advertising, more income and healthier profits. A man of his stature, wealth and power will always elicit widely diverse opinions and reactions. For my part I liked him. He was a straight shooter. He knew what he wanted and he knew how to get it.

A few years after the Wapping dispute had been consigned to history, there was a quirky link between my childhood and Murdoch's burgeoning media empire. He bought the Townsend Hook paper mill as part of the News International supply chain, and, when he launched Sky TV in the UK, he gave away free subscription packages to all the workers at the mill.

To think, if I'd still lived behind one of those brown doors in Snodland, I'd have ended up with a free satellite dish. I may have missed out on that one, but my career working with newspapers and magazines was only just beginning.

12

In the wake of Wapping

Nobody had the balls or foresight to do what Rupert Murdoch did. When he upped the stakes and declared war on union tyranny, the other Fleet Street proprietors were conspicuous by their absence. If Murdoch won, they would happily leech off his success and make their move into 21st-century print production. If he lost, they wouldn't be bloodied or have incurred the ire of the unions. Rupert won and, by default, so did all the other national titles. *The Guardian*, Associated Newspapers *(Daily Mail, Mail On Sunday & London Standard)*, United Newspapers *(Daily & Sunday Express)*, the *Financial Times*, the *Daily* and *Sunday Telegraph*, *The Observer* and Mirror Group Newspapers *(Daily Mirror, Sunday Mirror and Sunday People)* all shipped out of Fleet Street in Murdoch's slipstream. A further 7,000 print union jobs would be lost in the wake of Wapping. The mould had been well and truly shattered. It was a watershed moment for the print industry, a crippling blow for the unions and a land of opportunity for me and TNT Newsfast.

Proprietors wanted to speak with us but were still operating in a climate of fear in 1986. We'd have clandestine meetings and prepare the groundwork. Only later would we capitalise on the blueprint which was serving News International so well. The dispute officially ended on 5th February, 1987. It was the catalyst for me to start knocking on doors.

It's also an opportunity for me to share an eventful and amusing day spent 'selling' in Fleet Street with 'The Jones'. We had a busy day ahead. The first port of call was the *Express* for a 9am start. I'd travelled down to London Euston from Nuneaton, arriving at the offices in Fleet Street at 8.30am. The Circulation Director's secretary, a lady called Morag, spotted me outside. 'Morning, Tom, are you coming upstairs for a coffee before the meeting?'

'Thanks, Morag, but I'll just wait here for Alan. He'll be here in a minute and we'll be up.'

A couple of minutes later, Brian Bingham, the Assistant Circulation Director, arrived. 'Morning, Tom. Fancy coming up for a coffee?'

'Morning, Brian. Thanks, but I'll just wait for Alan to get here. It should be any minute now and we'll come up.'

It was pushing on for 9am when the Circulation Director, Nick Shot, walked up to the *Express* offices. 'Are you coming up, Tom? We need to start the meeting pretty promptly.'

'Morning, Nick. Alan should be here any minute and we'll be straight up – thanks.'

It'd gone nine o'clock. Where was The Jones? I looked down the street. I could see this Charlie Chaplin type figure, in a black overcoat, carrying what appeared to be a walking cane. It was Alan. What the hell did he have in his hand? It was the handbrake out of his Mercedes.

We dispensed with the pleasantries of the day. 'What the hell? What are you doing with your handbrake?' I asked.

'I wanted to show them why I'm late. I pulled on the handbrake and it came off in my hand,' said Alan, slightly out of breath.

This handbrake was covered in grease. I thought, what the bloody hell is he going to do with it? We went up the stairs. We were running late. As we approached the office I could hear Nick talking, 'Where the hell are TNT?' Brian said: 'Well, I saw Tom downstairs.' Morag chipped in, 'Yes he was here about half past eight.' We entered the room. Alan piped up, 'Sorry we're late. I had a problem with the car,' and plonked the slime-covered handbrake on top of Nick's leather inlay desk.

'Alan, would you take that 'thing' off my desk.' The disdain in Nick's voice could not have been any more obvious.

'Oh, yes, of course.' Alan picked it up and placed it in the umbrella stand. I watched as the gunk dripped off the handbrake and slid down the outside of the stand.

'Right! Can we get down to business?' said Nick. It was a rhetorical question, but Alan decided otherwise.

'Do you mind if I just go and wash my hands?'

'If you must,' said Nick in a resigned tone. Alan trotted off to the loo. He returned a few minutes later, this time with another question. 'I couldn't just borrow the phone could I, just to make a quick call?'

'Be my guest,' said Nick in sarcastic fashion.

I watched Alan punch the number into the keypad; it was going on forever. Surely he's not ringing bloody Australia? Yes, he was calling Australia. He was on the blower to Sir Peter for what seemed an age. Eventually he finished his 'quick' call.

Alan sat down. 'Right. Shall we get on with the meeting?'

Nick stared at him. If looks could kill, Alan would have been a dead man. 'You can do what you want. My board meeting starts in five minutes and that's where I'm going.' It wasn't the best way to start the day. As we were walking down the stairs Alan turned to me and, with puzzled innocence, said, 'Did I say something wrong?' You couldn't make it up, but that was Alan, incredibly focused in one sense, but a total lack of self awareness in another.

Next up was the *Financial Times* at the top of Ludgate Hill near St Paul's Cathedral. We jumped into a black cab. I only had a £20 note. Alan didn't have any cash on him. Not unusual for The Jones. The taxi driver didn't have any change. 'Have it on me, gents,' said the cabbie. The meeting went well. It helped that Alan didn't decorate the circulation director's desk with handbrake oil, or phone the other side of the world. We moved onto the *Daily Mail* and *Mail On Sunday* – but not without incident. It was lunchtime and every taxi was taken. Having been late once, Alan was determined it wasn't going to happen again.

'Come on, let's get a bus; it'll be quicker,' he said.

'Don't be daft, I've only got a £20 note and you haven't got any money on you. We can't get the bus. Let's wait for a taxi.'

'No, no,' said Alan, 'we're going to be late.' At that moment one of the old London Routemaster buses – with the open platform and pole on the back – dawdled past in the heavy traffic. Alan jumped on. I stood and watched as the bus slowly descended Ludgate Hill. I was still watching when Alan came flying off the bus, with a big black bus conductor waving his fist at him. Of course, he didn't have any money to pay his fare, did he?

'Where did you get to?' said Alan, all out of puff. 'You were too quick for me,' I lied, somehow managing not to laugh. We caught a cab to the *Mail* – I paid.

We were well received at both the *Mail* and later *The Guardian* – everybody was interested in how we were working with News International, with no lack of admiration for the job we'd done and were continuing to do. It was now edging up to 5pm and I was about to head back to Euston.

'My keys! Where are my car keys?' Alan may have had the handbrake to his Merc, but not his keys. We headed back into the offices of *The Guardian*. Alan turned the Circulation Director's office upside down looking for those bloody keys. We checked the gents' and the reception – no sign of them anywhere.

'There's only one thing for it – we'll have to retrace our footsteps and go back to everywhere we've been today,' said Alan.

'Well, you can, but I'm catching the train back to Nuneaton.'

'But my car! It's in the car park. I can't just leave it,' said The Jones.

'Maybe you left the keys in the car?' I suggested. 'I wouldn't worry, it'll still be there – it hasn't got a handbrake, for a start.' This was my way of expressing empathy! To this day, I can't actually recall if he found his car keys that night or how he got home, or indeed if he got home. Next time we speak, I'll have to ask him. Alan was a top, top bloke and very astute, but he could drive you mad, in the nicest possible way. One example was a meeting we had with Brian Horwite, the Circulation Director for News International, in the wake of our Wapping success. The Jones and I wanted to know if there was any extra business to be had.

Brian was exploring a few possible avenues. Alan was keen to mop up any new opportunities. It didn't seem to matter what Brian said, Alan's reply was, 'We can do that. We can do that, can't we, Tom?' He'd kick my ankle each and every time to ensure my nodding agreement. He must have done it half a dozen times in the space of 45 minutes. As we were leaving, Brian shook my hand and said, 'How's your ankle, Tom?' Alan's interpretation of 'unobtrusive' wasn't always the best.

The first big post-Wapping breakthrough came in July 1987. We negotiated with *The Telegraph*'s Circulation Director, Chris Haslam, and picked up the contract to distribute *The Daily Telegraph* and *Sunday Telegraph*, from their new printing plant on the Isle of Dogs. We could combine some deliveries with the News International titles, making us more efficient and profitable.

Whereas our negotiations with *The Telegraph* and News International had been professional and respectful, our dealings with Murdoch's main rival in the tabloid wars were anything but. Robert Maxwell was the antithesis of Murdoch. Rupert was a bloke I admired, and respected. It was a real buzz observing him in the work environment and a pleasure to know him. I never worked with Maxwell and I'm bloody glad of the fact. He was a bully and a crook – as was discovered after his death in November 1991. As the owner of a publishing empire which included Mirror Group Newspapers, he stole hundreds of millions of pounds from his companies' pension funds.

I was in Marks & Spencer in Leicester's Fosse Shopping Park on a Saturday morning when The Jones contacted me.

'Maxwell wants to see us,' said Alan, in an excited voice.

'Great!' This was good news. 'When?' I asked.

'This afternoon, at the *Mirror* in London.'

'This afternoon?' Shit. Nothing like a bit of advanced warning, and this was nothing like it.

Alan immediately raised my hopes when he said, 'Yes, he's offered to send his personal helicopter to get us down there.'

Great again – I wasn't against being whisked down to London in Maxwell's helicopter. Alan soon killed that idea.

'But I said there was no need. We'd drive down instead.' Bollocks! No helicopter ride for me.

We arrived at the Mirror Group headquarters. Maxwell's office – rather like his ego and his waistline – was huge. There was screen after screen after screen displaying global stock market prices. It was a sight to behold. The carpet was of an incredible depth – almost as deep as the debts Maxwell ran up prior to his drowning in the Atlantic Ocean – with the shag pile curling up and over our shoes.

Dispensing with anything even approaching a 'Good Afternoon', Maxwell bellowed, 'Give me a price.' The meeting hadn't even begun. His was a different approach, to say the least.

'We'd need to know your tonnage size and print runs before we can give you a price,' I said.

'You already bloody know. You'll have done your research. I want a price within 24 hours.' It was impossible not to take an instant dislike to the man. We'd heard all the stories, how he was forever bawling at his people, berating and belittling them.

He was abhorrent, thoroughly deserving of his reputation as a tyrant, a man who revelled in other people's discomfort and misfortune. Clearly, we wouldn't be entering into any form of constructive dialogue with the megalomaniac from the *Mirror*.

It was left to Maxwell's Chief of Staff, Peter Jay, the former UK Ambassador to the United States, to restore some semblance of sanity to what had deteriorated into a very strange Saturday afternoon. Exercising all his diplomatic skills, Jay ushered us away from his odious employer. He asked that we prepare an outline proposal and be in a position to deliver it to Maxwell's country pile, Headington Hill Hall in Oxfordshire, at 10am on the Sunday. Far from impressed, but still wanting to gain the *Mirror's* business, Alan and I went straight back to Atherstone and drafted a proposal.

The next morning we drove to what we thought would be a second, and somewhat more productive, meeting with Maxwell. We arrived on time and were shown to a waiting area. Obviously he wasn't ready to start on time. As we waited, Jim Smith, the then manager of the Maxwell-owned Oxford United Football Club, arrived. He went straight upstairs. Moments later we heard Maxwell's booming voice, 'You're fired.' Smith came down the stairs and walked straight out of the building. His three-year reign as Oxford's manager was over. Unlike Smith, we didn't actually get to see Maxwell that day.

We didn't know it at the time, but he was using Newsfast as a stalking horse to get a better deal out of a rival distributor. Having our proposal displayed on his desk, and Alan and me inside Headington Hill Hall, gave him extra leverage with our competitors. It was a deceitful, but clever, move. We didn't get the business.

It was left to Jay to diplomatically tell us Maxwell couldn't see us. We'd inadvertently served our purpose, our presence no longer required. We were never going to win the contract in the first place.

Maxwell notwithstanding, we were doing well and picking up business in the newspaper sector, but I also wanted to break into the magazine market. It was huge; the potential was massive. It took two years, but when it came it was well worth the wait.

Heavy snowfall in the winter of 1989 led to many parts of the country being impassable, especially in rural areas. We had contingency plans in place with farmers in known cold weather 'trouble spots' – arrangements that would later help me to tell a big lie and land a major deal.

The farmers received a one-off payment from TNT in return for rescuing any of our wagons stuck in snow within a stipulated radius of the farmer's land. It paid off handsomely. We were the only ones who managed to get through to all the wholesalers during the snowdrifts. Our competitors – Robert Maxwell's Newsflow – didn't. It caught the attention of EMAP – the country's second largest magazine publisher.

EMAP's Circulation Director, Trevor Peach, rang me and asked how we managed to reach wholesalers on the Isle of Thanet. I told him that we'd used a helicopter. It was a barefaced lie, but he believed me. EMAP were still having their products transported by rail, so they were a prime target for us. I was asked to go and see Kevin Hand the managing director.

We hit it off immediately. He told me why he was considering switching to road deliveries.

'I was standing on Peterborough Station. It was absolutely pissing down and I spotted a roll cage packed full of my magazines. It was parked or abandoned on a platform right beneath some broken guttering. The water was pouring onto the magazines and nobody gave a shit.' He liked my proposal and we signed the contract that night. Other major publishers soon followed: Seymour Press, Haymarket Publications and the *Radio Times*. It was great for TNT Newsfast. The magazines were all destined for wholesalers where we were already delivering the newspapers. We would incur few or no extra overheads. We were into the realms of pure profit. The *Radio Times*, in particular, was a landmark contract and incredibly prestigious. The Jones and I sealed the deal when we went, armed with our proposal, to see the Circulation Director, Les Burr, in central London.

We drove there in Alan's Mercedes – this time complete with handbrake – and parked. Alan only had a tenner on him, so he nipped into a shop to get some change. He came out and slotted five £1 coins into the meter. I said, 'The bloke who owns that Toyota is going to love you.'

'Why, what do you mean?' said Alan.

'Because you've just fed his fucking meter for the rest of the day.' The Jones had filled the wrong meter. He popped back into the shop, changed his £5 note and proceeded to pump another fiver's worth of coins into the correct meter. It turned out to be £10 well spent.

We were now by far and away the leader in the market. It was all being achieved on the back of what we'd done at Wapping. Murdoch had been the big winner but, in our own way, we weren't far behind.

Wagons roll – TNT Newsfast trucks on the ramp inside Fortress Wapping, with Tower Bridge in the background.

Me (left) with Tony Sim (centre). I never quite worked out if Simbo was a genius or a madman.

Family affair at the Palace. Amy, Gina, me and Scott
with my treasured OBE Medal.

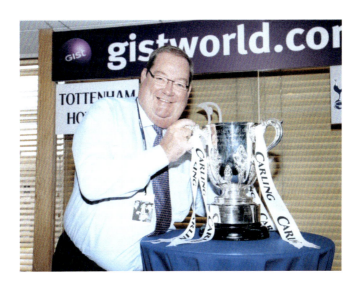

Me and the League Cup – Carling Cup –
one of the numerous cups I've been fortunate to see Spurs
win since I began supporting them in the early 1960s.

My son Scott and daughter-in-law Kim had a
fairytale wedding at St Paul's Cathedral.

Rupert Murdoch with the first editions of *The Sun* and *The Times* produced at Wapping on the night of Sunday 26th January, 1986.

Me and 'The Jones'.

Picket line violence at Wapping @John Sturrock/report digital.co.uk

Father of the Bride, and Amy was a beautiful bride.

Me and 'Atky'.

Me and Peter Nichol, the man who introduced
the Wooden Spoon into my life.

Showtime at The Lido in Paris. Bill Hanley is standing in front of me, with 'The Jones' and 'Atky' to his right, after TNT were declared European Quality Award winners.

Dad and Mum – Charles and Cathie Bell.

Gina's mum, Marie Vincent, with Tottenham goal-scoring legend Martin Chivers, at my OBE Luncheon at the Landmark Hotel.

Limited Edition – one of only 12 copies to ever exist of TNT's proposal to Rupert Murdoch.

13

Spurs

I'd been preparing to watch Spurs against Real Madrid on the night I was first told about the exciting, and ultimately career-changing, opportunity, to support Rupert Murdoch's operations. Ordinarily I'd have been supremely pissed off to miss such a big European clash, but work had come first and rightly so. We'd gone on to achieve a huge result at Fortress Wapping, unlike Spurs, who ended up losing 1-0 to the Spaniards. Skipper Steve Perryman had scored an own goal. I hadn't missed much. It was the first time Tottenham had lost at home in European competition. It didn't get any better in the return leg. Perryman was sent off and Madrid went on to win the UEFA Cup that season.

When The Jones rolled up at White Hart Lane with the big reveal about Murdoch, I'd been supporting Spurs for more than 20 years. I was what you'd call a 'proper' fan. I'd go and watch my team whatever the weather, no matter where they were in the league table. Yes, it helped that I'd started following them in their pomp in the early 60s, but I was no glory hunter. I was there for the long haul. I was, however, very lucky that my employers were also the sponsors of my team. In football parlance that was a *result!*

People assume that TNT's long-standing commercial relationship with Spurs was initially down to me. It wasn't. The irony is that the man who sealed the first deal with Spurs was no friend of mine. It was Don Dick, the only dissenting voice among the TNT hierarchy when the News International deal landed in our lap. I never liked the man. I suspect he didn't much care for me either, but I do owe him that one debt of gratitude, albeit indirectly.

He saw the benefits of investing in customer hospitality at a top English football club. Why Spurs were chosen, I don't know, but I was glad they were. Don's original approach to the club would have seen TNT become Tottenham's first-ever shirt sponsors. The proposal also included the leasing of two corporate boxes at White Hart Lane, one for TNT's domestic business, the other to host customers of TNT International. As it was, the brewery company, Holsten Pils, offered more money for the shirt sponsorship, but Don retained the two boxes. I'll freely admit it was manna from heaven that my employers had access to such great facilities – even more so when I was calling the shots. Whoever would have thought that the kid who used to bring his own wooden stool to the matches would one day end up in the 'posh seats' at every home game. Mixing business with football was one of the biggest perks of my job. It put my dad's whisky-filled teapot from the Kirkcaldy distillery somewhat in the shade.

It was by no means a North London indulgence. We'd invite customers from all over the country, depending on who Spurs were playing. If it was Manchester City or Manchester United, we'd invite those served by our two Manchester depots; if it was Liverpool or Everton, they'd be drawn from Merseyside; if it was Aston Villa, Birmingham, Wolves or West Brom, they'd come from the West Midlands. It worked a treat every time, irrespective of whether the visiting team won, lost or drew. It was a good day out with fine food, a few drinks, good conversation and cementing ties with valued customers. We had a winning formula.

Of course, I'd always be rooting for a home win. It was scant consolation to see a customer ecstatic at the end of a match if the price was a Spurs defeat. Over the years I sought to balance my Tottenham tribalism with an exemplary approach to customer care. I don't think I ever quite managed it. Obviously it paid to keep the customers happy. Part of the 'match day experience' was to have celebrities attend games. Of course, we'd see some of the players and plenty of ex-players and managers, but we'd often be in the same room as celebrities: TV actors, musicians, comedians; it was an eclectic mix. It helped to know who these people were, but things didn't always run true to form.

I was hosting customers at one game, and TNT's newly appointed Events Co-ordinator Katie Strode spotted an unkempt, dishevelled figure in the suite. Bedecked in shorts and open-toed sandals, the man wasn't exactly a picture of sartorial elegance. Suspecting he was some sort of freeloader, Katie approached him. 'Excuse me. My boss is hosting a corporate event – you can't come in here dressed like that.'

'Don't you know who I am?' asked the man.

'No, I don't. Should I?' asked a quizzical Katie.

'I'm Alf Garnett,' came the explanation.

'Who?' Katie was none the wiser.

'I'm Alf Garnett off the television. I'm Warren Mitchell. I play Alf Garnett in *Till Death Us Do Part*. I'm here to do the warm-up act before the match,' he said, grinning at the clearly unimpressed Katie.

'Well, I still don't know who you are.'

Katie came over to me. 'That bloke over there says he's someone called Alf Garnett and he's here to do the warm-up?' It was a question rather than a statement. I looked across at 'Alf'. He nodded and I nodded back. I said to Katie, 'Yes, that's Alf Garnett. He'll be hilarious, you wait and see.'

He was very funny – as I'd expected – and over the years we became good friends. I hadn't realised what a massive Spurs fan he was – of course, his Alf Garnett character was a big West Ham fan. Sometimes fiction can get in the way of reality. Sadly, Warren became too ill to get down to the games and he died in 2015.

I once had the pleasure of having lunch with Bill Nicholson, the manager of Spurs' double winning team of 1960-61, and the first man to lead an English club to European success – Spurs won the European Cup Winners Cup in 1963. He was a great manager and a remarkable chap.

I was sitting next to him and he asked me who I thought was the best passer of the ball at the club. I said, 'John White.'

Bill said, 'No.'

I said, 'Danny Blanchflower.'

Bill said, 'No.'

I couldn't think. I'd just said two of the finest passers of a ball in Tottenham's history. 'I don't know, in that case. Who?'

Bill said, 'Jimmy Greaves.'

I thought, *Jimmy Greaves?* 'He's our centre forward; how could he be the best passer of a ball?'

Bill gave me a knowing grin. 'You just watch how he passes the ball into the corner of the net. He never shoots; he passes it past the keeper.' The next time I saw Jimmy Greaves play I watched him very closely when he scored. Bill was spot on.

Bill was credited with saying, 'It is better to fail aiming high than to succeed aiming low. We of Spurs have set our sights very high, so high in fact that failure will have in it an echo of glory.' I've always thought that was a pretty good maxim for anything in life.

Being a regular in Spurs' top hospitality suite – The Oak Room – meant I got to know and become firm friends with Martin Chivers, Tottenham's record signing from Southampton for £125,000 back in 1968. Years later, in 2010, Martin would be among my guests at a special lunch after I'd received the OBE at Buckingham Palace.

Steve Perryman – whose own goal and sending off against Real Madrid had helped scupper our hopes of UEFA Cup glory in 1985 – was a tremendous bloke. He ended up winning six trophies with Spurs – two FA Cups, two League Cups twice and the UEFA Cup twice. I met him after a game once and asked him if he'd give his autograph to my son, Scott. Steve said, 'Give me five minutes and I'll be back.'

I'd heard that 'I'll be back in five minutes' line before, from other big names in football. They never came back. I wasn't impressed. I couldn't have been more wrong. Steve returned, only this time with a Polaroid camera. They were all the rage back in the day. You could take a picture and the image would emerge from the back of the camera within a couple of minutes. Steve had his photo taken with little Scott and then signed the back of the picture.

'Now you'll be able to go into school and show all your mates the proof that you met me here at Tottenham,' said Steve. It was a lovely gesture and one which meant the world to Scott.

I've been privileged to rub shoulders with all the great and the good at White Hart Lane for more than two decades. Dave Mackay, one of the double winning team of 1961, was a fearsome Scottish warrior on the pitch, but the mildest and measured of men off it. Softly spoken and courteous, you wouldn't believe it was the same man.

Cliff Jones, another double winner, and a Welsh wizard on the left wing, is a truly remarkable man. Now aged 84, Cliff was a match day host at all the games during my time with TNT. He celebrated his 77th birthday by doing 77 press-ups in one of the suites. Italian giants, Juventus, once offered £100,000 for him, but Bill Nicholson didn't even consider it. I can't begin to imagine what the equivalent price would be in today's crazily inflated transfer market. Cliff told me the story of how he was given a pay rise when the maximum player wage was abolished in the 1960s. He was earning £14 a week in the season and £10 a week during the summer, when Bill Nicholson called him into his office.

Cliff said, 'Bill told me he was putting me up to £20 a week, all year round. I was gobsmacked. I got on the bus to go home and it was still only one shilling and three pence. I told my wife about the pay rise and we decided we were going to buy our first house!'

What struck me about the tale was Cliff's humility and how 'normal' footballers were in his day. It was a world removed from the overpaid, cosseted multi-millionaires of nowadays. Another Tottenham legend – Ricardo Villa – was an equally modest guy. He had a pre-match meal with me and TNT's guests and was an absolute delight. Ricky – as he is known – had won the World Cup with his native Argentina in 1978. Three years later he scored the most amazing winning goal, as Spurs beat Manchester City 3-2 in the FA Cup Final replay.

The first match had finished 1-1 on the Saturday afternoon. The replay on the night of Thursday 14th May drew a 92,000 capacity crowd. I was lucky enough to attend both games. Ricky opened the scoring in the eighth minute. City equalised three minutes later and then took the lead early in the second half. Spurs levelled in the 70th minute. Six minutes later, Ricky produced his magical, mazy run and we won the Cup.

Such was the quality of his winner – he dribbled the ball past four defenders before slotting it past City keeper Joe Corrigan – it was acclaimed as the Wembley Goal of the Century at the turn of the millennium.

I was normally accompanied to Spurs games by a guy called Jon Stockton. Jon worked for me and was Tottenham mad. His football hero was Ricky Villa, but he hadn't been able to get to this particular match.

'I know somebody who will be really disappointed about today,' I said to Ricky.

'Who's that?' he asked. 'Why would they be upset?'

'It's a guy called Jon Stockton. You're his hero and he couldn't make it today. He'll be gutted when he finds out you were on our table.'

Quick as a flash, Ricky said, 'Have you got his phone number? I will speak with him.' He was on the phone to Jon for the next 10 minutes. 'Stockie' couldn't believe it. It was a really thoughtful thing to do.

Ricky remarked on the contrast in how he was welcomed at Spurs and how his former club treated him back in Argentina. 'Every time I return to Tottenham I am made to feel like a king. I have a seat in the Director's Box and lovely hospitality.

'I go on the pitch at half time and get a wonderful reception from the fans. They sing my name. They remember the good times we enjoyed together.

'When I go to my old club in Argentina, they give me the cheapest seat at the back of the stand. They virtually ignore me.' He was so easy-going and great company for me and the TNT customers. He gave me his address, a ranch in Buenos Aires, and told me I was welcome to visit anytime I was in Argentina. What's more, he meant it. 10 years later I did finally get to Argentina, but didn't take him up on his offer – maybe I should have done.

Beating City at Wembley was one of the best nights I've had as a Spurs fan. Losing to City in another FA Cup replay was one of the most bizarre. The author of this book – David Walker – had joined TNT in the summer of 2003. He was a City fan so we had a £20 bet on the FA Cup 4th round tie in early 2004. Once again, the first game had ended 1-1. This time the replay was at White Hart Lane. Goals by Ledley King, Robbie Keane and Christian Ziege had given Spurs a 3-0 lead after the first 45 minutes. City then had a man sent off for dissent during the half time interval. I was hosting clients in The Oak Room – the best hospitality suite – when I received a text from David asking if I'd take a cheque. Clearly both he and I believed the game was both won and lost. I told him I'd take cash only. Quite incredibly, City's 10 men scored four unanswered goals in the second half, with the winner coming in injury time. I paid up the next day, but we decided the £20 would be best served going to a children's charity called the Wooden Spoon. It made defeat a fraction more palatable.

I've seen Spurs win three FA Cups, four League Cups and two UEFA Cups, and I'd like to see them win a good many more trophies in the years to come.

14

Doing the business

'You're bored.' It was Bill Hanley ringing me.

'No, I'm not bored, Bill,' I replied. I was surprised he'd even suggested I was bored. Why would I be bored?

He repeated, 'You're bored.'

'No, seriously, I'm not bored, the job's going well.'

'I know. That's why you're bored,' said Bill.

My protestations clearly weren't getting through. 'No, no, Bill. I assure you, I'm alright.'

'Alright, then, lad, I'll leave you to it. Just phone me when you realise you're bored.'

I put the receiver down. What a strange phone call. Why would I be bored? TNT Newsfast had made all the right headlines over our involvement at Wapping, we were the market sector leaders and we were making pots of money. I was in my element.

The next day I was at my desk for my usual 7am start. I reviewed the overnight reports from Wapping, Kinning Park and *The Telegraph*. Everything was as sweet as a nut. No picketing, no aggro, no police briefings – no bother.

A week or so passed. Something was missing. There was no adrenaline surge. Running the Newsfast business was easy – at least it was by my standards – too easy. The days were taking longer to get through. I picked up the phone to Bill. 'You were right. I'm bored.' The sage-like Lancastrian at the other end of the line said, 'I knew you'd get there soon enough. Come to The Belfry tonight. We'll talk business over a bit of dinner.'

TNT Newsfast was my baby. It'd been a rollercoaster ride, one that I wouldn't have missed for the world – even that night when I'd stood on the ramp at Wapping, tears in my eyes, almost dead on my feet. Only by experiencing the desperate lows can you truly appreciate the giddying highs. Without realising it, I'd become very comfortable in my role. I needed a new challenge.

'I want you to take over the 'parcels' – are you interested?' asked Bill. The 'parcels' was the cornerstone of the TNT empire. Was I interested? Christ, yes, I was interested. Bill explained that the UK & Ireland parcels operation was making an annual profit of £4million but – and it was a big but – that profit margin was essentially coming from just one source – IPEC – the international division of TNT. The UK business undertook collections and deliveries for IPEC, resulting in a £4 million 're-charge'. This was effectively the only source of 'profit'.

It meant the rest of TNT parcels were barely breaking even. It had to change. It was down to me to instigate that change. One thing was certain – I wasn't going to be bored. 'When do I start?' Bill's reply shouldn't have come as a surprise, 'Tomorrow – you've a meeting with all your Regional General Managers. I won't bother attending; you can handle it.'

I was given responsibility for two-thirds of TNT's range of parcels operations – four divisions: TNT Tristar, TNT Supamail, AM Express and TNT Overnite. I'd been the National Sales Manager for Tristar – a three-day delivery service – and I hadn't enjoyed it. The other three divisions were much of a muchness, all ostensibly doing the same thing, barring a few tweaks and refinements – delivering next day mail. It was obvious there was a lot of duplication of effort, too many overheads and not enough focus on best practice.

Bill had told me of widespread unrest among the field sales people. They were complaining about the poor quality of the appointments being fed through from the telesales teams.

I said, 'We can soon change that. Let the field sales people make their own appointments. Give them one day a week off the road and they can sort their own business diaries.'

'So, what will you do with all the telesales people?' asked Bill.

I answered a question with a question. 'How many mailshots do we do, and how many of those mailshots receive follow-up calls? If, as I suspect, we're not doing enough, that's how we deploy our tellers.' That wasn't bad going, considering I hadn't even started the job.

Just one meeting with the Regional General Managers told me the business needed an injection of new ideas, fresh thinking and dynamism. It was crying out for energy, youth and vitality. These divisions had been allowed to stagnate. They were populated with people who were quite happy to keep their heads down, do their last few years and then walk off with their company pension. They weren't cutting it and I wasn't having it.

By contrast, one of the first jobs I had to do was stop a key man resigning from TNT.

Chris Atkinson – the man I'd succeeded as National Sales Manager for Tristar – had handed in his resignation on news of my appointment.

It wasn't anything personal against me. On the contrary, we both liked and respected each other. Maybe Chris thought he should have had the promotion. I couldn't be sure of his reasons. All I knew was, here was a guy who could be a tremendous asset to me in my new role. The last thing I wanted was him walking out the door before I'd even started. I had many fine days in my 33 years at TNT, none finer than the day I persuaded him to stay. Together, we'd forge a success story spanning the next 15 years.

As a major player in the industry, TNT was, as you'd expect, geared up with the latest technology – scanners, conveyor belts and all manner of sophisticated sorting equipment. The automated systems were designed and equipped to carry what I'd describe as 'standard' parcels – boxes and packages of a certain size and weight – compatible with our machines. To my horror I uncovered a trend – and a growing one at that – where items couldn't go through our automated processes. We were carrying stuff such as ladders, unwrapped metal goods and pallets of God knows what. They were incompatible, unwieldy, time-consuming and non-profit-making. They were a pain. They had to go.

I imposed restrictions on what we were prepared to transport. Regional General Managers and General Managers were left in no doubt as to what we would and wouldn't handle. TNT had been busy fools for far too long. Those that ignored, or tried to get around, my new edict, soon came a cropper. I was very 'hands on'. I'd be present late at night, when trailers, from all over the UK, would arrive at our central sortation centre – the hub in Atherstone. If they were carrying 'incompatibles' I'd return the goods to the offending depots.

The Regional General Manager (RGM) would get a call from me at two, three or four o'clock in the morning, telling them the 'shit' they'd sent to the hub was on its way back. I'd ring at that unearthly time of the day for one good reason. Not only would I wake up the RGM, I'd more than likely wake his wife up at the same time. He'd be getting a bollocking off me and more than likely grief off his 'missus' if her beauty sleep kept on being interrupted. They soon got the message. They could also deal with any backlash from irate customers, pacify them and try to keep them on board with TNT. It was their problem. I was there to make money. We were no longer carrying items where we couldn't make a profit.

I hadn't been in the job for long when we lost a long-standing contract with the Ministry of Defence. It had been worth £100,000 a week, in excess of £5 million a year. On the face of it, it was a big blow. The following week the revenue had dropped by the £100k, but the profits had gone up. Obviously what was perceived to be a prestigious piece of business was actually an unprofitable waste of time and energy. It proved that looks could be deceptive to the untrained eye.

I was also there to ensure the cash flowed in on time. When I took over we were dealing with a backlog of 18,000 invoice queries. We'd be resolving them at a rate of 4,000 each week, only to find another 4,000 had cropped up. We were drowning in a sea of invoice queries. The money should've been flooding in. It was coming in at a trickle. I attended a meeting with TNT's auditor KPMG, and Reg Bailey, the Head Auditor, left me in no doubt. The problem with the invoices was out of control. Change was needed and needed immediately.

I asked Chris why we were having all these problems? How and why had they been allowed to mount up?

Chris investigated. Customer discounts were a huge bone of contention. TNT had been offering all kinds of different discounts, some at the discretion of the sales reps, some sanctioned by depot General Managers, some by Head Office. It was a mess. We were bogged down in paperwork. We were arguing with our customers. It was killing the company. We weren't having any problems with customers who paid a flat rate; no ambiguity existed. It was all to do with the myriad of weird and not so wonderful discounts.

I had to take action – action that many would see as draconian. I stopped the discounts. If discounts didn't exist there wouldn't be any haggling over which discount should or shouldn't apply. 'Discount' would cease to be a word in the TNT vocabulary. Chris devised a new, and fair, flat-rate schedule. There would be no more dalliances with discounts. We provided the service, the customer paid the bill. No ifs or buts.

When Chris addressed the TNT National Sales Conference, the delegates were completely disbelieving. They couldn't comprehend a policy of no discounts to customers. Murmurings of discontent reverberated throughout the hall. I was sitting next to Alan Jones, listening to an audience of hundreds of salesmen and women who thought they were right and I was wrong. The Jones couldn't contain his delight. Discount was a dirty, horrible, filthy word by his reckoning.

Discounts had always been given. Discounts were one of the essential 'tools' of their trade. This new bloke, *this Tom Bell*, couldn't be serious. He would soon change his tune when his master plan failed to deliver. I could almost see the defiance in their eyes – they knew best.

They didn't. A no-discount policy quickly translated into next-to-no invoice queries, rising revenue streams and increasing profits.

By the time I'd completed my review and restructuring of the TNT divisions, I'd shut down one and amalgamated the other three. Tristar was the first to go. A three-day delivery service wasn't the future and would soon become a relic of the past. The closure heralded a new 'clear deck' policy. Whatever came in to a depot went out within 24 hours. It'd never happened before.

We cherry-picked the best Tristar customers, persuaded them it was worth paying the extra for a one-day delivery service and retained their custom. I wasn't interested in the rest. It wouldn't turn a profit. Anyone wanting a three-day service was dumped.

It made no sense running Overnite, AM Express and Supamail as separate brands. They were all quintessentially the same. I put it to The Jones and Bill that we should form a new, all-encompassing division. It'd be more efficient, there'd be a massive drop in overhead costs and we'd increase revenue and profits. Alan and Bill agreed. TNT Express was born.

There were two remaining TNT divisions not under my wing – TNT Parcel Office and TNT Sameday. I was to 'gain' Parcel Office in unusual circumstances. Along with Alan and Chris, I was attending a Parcel Office sales conference. It was a shambolic affair. Ken Young, the Divisional General Manager, and Geoff Dobson, his Sales Manager, were on stage. It was excruciatingly bad. I was sitting on the front row of the audience with The Jones and Atky. Alan kicked me and whispered, 'You and Atky get up on that stage and save this thing.' I said, 'No, it's nothing to do with me.'

Alan persisted in tapping me on the shin. 'Get on that stage!'

'No, Alan. They're not my divisions. They're not my responsibility.'

'Tom, get up there and bloody do something! Talk about anything; just do something.'

'No! I'm not doing it!' I was adamant.

The normally restrained Jones was almost ready to combust. 'Right, from now on, from this minute, you're responsible for Parcel Office.'

I nudged Chris. 'Come on, Atky, we're going up on the stage.'

'Why?' said Chris. 'We're not responsible for Parcel Office.'

'We are now,' I responded. 'Alan's just put me in charge.' The two of us made our unexpected appearance on the stage, and ad-libbed and brightened the place up with a little bit of humour and some motivational chit-chat.

The next morning I called Ken Young into my office. 'Here's a blank piece of paper.'

'Yes,' agreed Ken.

'Yes, I want you to write your resignation on it.'

'Resignation?' said a clearly perplexed Ken.

'Yes, Ken. That sales conference yesterday was a total embarrassment. You're not for me.'

Clearly shocked, Ken said, 'Well, that's a pity because I quite like you.'

'I'm sorry, Ken, you've got to go. It just won't work, and while you're at it you can get Geoff to tender his resignation as well.' Parcel Office was a big loss maker. It was bleeding us dry. It didn't take long for me to decide to shut it down.

TNT Sameday – the same-day delivery service (the clue's in the name) – was completely different. It was making good money. TNT Express and TNT Sameday were a perfect fit. From making just £4 million a year, I would soon be running a business clearing

£3 million a week. It would be profits with a capital 'P'. Our return on sales would average 6% to 7% at a time when the rest of the industry was running between 2% and 3%. We were consistently outstripping the market. We weren't the cheapest, but we were the best. People were prepared to pay for a truly premium service and we would provide it. We expanded and invested. I oversaw the opening of strategic new depots in Edinburgh, Glasgow, Preston, Leeds, Rotherham, Birmingham, Crawley and Swansea, as well as a state-of-the-art sortation hub at Kingsbury, just down the road from Atherstone.

The additional geographical presence enhanced our profile in the market and contributed to my two main priorities – maximising profits and optimising customer care. I also applied an invaluable lesson learned off none other than Rupert Murdoch. I was sitting with Rupert in Fortress Wapping, and I asked him what his approach was to marketing.

He said, 'Do you remember as a child, if you threw a snowball against a wall some of it would stick and some of it would fall to the ground? It'd be the same with every snowball thrown, but if you threw enough snowballs you'd eventually cover the wall. That's my philosophy.'

With this in mind we would send out hundreds of thousands of mailshots to our prospective customers. Some would hit the target and stick. Others would fall on stony ground. One time we experimented and eased off to see what would happen. The result was a drop in business. We went back to throwing lots and lots of snowballs.

Ours was an intensely competitive market with a host of domestic rivals, as well as global giants DHL, UPS and FedEx. I encouraged that competitive spirit within the ranks of TNT to help create a stronger mindset among our people.

We had league tables for what we called 'The Perfect Transaction', a process whereby every element of the booking, payment, collection and delivery of a consignment was fulfilled to perfection. Depots the length and breadth of the UK and Ireland would be competing against each other, to see who could generate the highest revenue, who had the best customer service score, and which teams were hitting their key performance indicators (KPIs). It was transparent, it was monitored and it was healthy. You had to be a winner to survive and prosper in TNT.

The Jones championed a culture of 'continuous improvement'. Everything was based on being the best that we could be. Quality was of paramount importance. One way of demonstrating that you're the best of the best is by seeking, and gaining, third party endorsement. External awards and recognition became a key element in our selling proposition.

The Oscars of the express parcels industry were, and still are, the Motor Transport Awards. *Motor Transport* magazine was, and still is, one of the most authoritative and respected commentators in the road transport sector. In my two decades at the top of TNT Express we won an unprecedented 21 Motor Transport Awards.

When the words, 'And the winner is… TNT' were announced at the annual awards ceremony in London's Grosvenor House Hotel, a crescendo of boos would erupt. We were despised and admired in equal measure. Our competitors hated us winning. Behind closed doors they couldn't help but respect our professionalism and our achievements.

Some regarded us as shallow and egotistical, but they were missing the point. Yes, of course it was great picking up awards and all the accompanying plaudits, but there was more to it than that, much more.

Every award submission was backed up by a review of all the relevant business processes. It would extol our strengths but, more importantly, it would expose any weaknesses. We would rectify any shortcomings. In effect, each entry became a means to improving how we went about our work. This would show up in the financials or customer satisfaction ratings. There was definite method in our insatiable madness for awards.

That said, when The Jones entered us for the European Quality Award, my initial reaction was, 'Great! More bloody work!' Those feelings soon evaporated. Both me and Atky supported the entry, knowing full well that it could only improve the company, as well as give us a shot at a very prestigious award. We won the European Quality Prize – the runners-up slot – two times on the bounce. It was good, but not good enough. We won the actual Quality Award at the third time of asking. In football terms it was like we'd scooped the Champions League. The Motor Transport Awards were akin to winning the Premier League – we did that all the time. Not only were we big hitters in our own sector, we now had household names such as Tesco and Royal Bank of Scotland wanting to learn from us. We'd gone to the next level. We'd undertake 'Quality Tours' in the USA, with Chris and I sharing and learning best practice with huge Stateside brands located in New York, Chicago, Cleveland, Los Angeles and San Francisco, to name but a few.

We were on a roll like never before, but change was on its way. Our swashbuckling, pioneering ways, born of our Australian heritage, were about to be torn away. The Dutch were taking over. It was like swapping the thrill of the Aussie surf for a dyke in the Netherlands. Things would never be the same again.

15

Australia fair

Sydney is one of my favourite places in the world. I know it better than I know Nuneaton – and I've lived on the outskirts of the North Warwickshire town for the past 35 years. Resplendent with its iconic Opera House, stunning Harbour Bridge and beautiful Bondi Beach, I simply love the place. In truth, I love Australia – the culture, the climate, the food – and I loved working for the people who used to own and run TNT.

I'd had some truly memorable moments alongside one of Australia's favourite sons – Rupert Murdoch – and TNT's global bosses, men of the calibre of Sir Peter Abeles and Ross Cribb, were a class apart. They'd blazed a trail across the face of the earth and made TNT a world renowned and highly respected business. They were the embodiment of all that was good Down Under – they were grafters and innovators. They were fearless men with fire in their bellies. They were risk takers and they knew how to live life. They were definitely my kind of people.

My first experience of Australia came in 1987 after TNT Newsfast's successful collaboration with Murdoch and News International. All those weeks away from my family, the sleep deprivation, the stresses and strains of Fortress Wapping, hadn't gone unnoticed nearly 11,000 miles away in Sydney.

Sir Peter had been delighted how we'd weathered the picket lines, helped his mate Murdoch through troubled times and cornered a new and profitable market in newspaper distribution. My reward was an invitation to attend TNT's Annual General Meeting in Sydney, before spending some quality time on a break with Gina.

It was such a thrill to be there among the company's main men, Sir Peter, Ross, Don Dick, The Jones, Bill Hanley and the various TNT Managing Directors from so many different countries. In all honesty I felt out of my depth. These guys were the real powerbrokers. I was just happy being along for the ride. I was the new boy on the block and my presentation on Newsfast's rapid growth was well received by the Board. My star was rising, but it was nowhere near the dizzying heights of Sir Peter's. Australia's biggest selling national newspaper *The Australian* had just named him 'Australian of the Year'.

It was no mean feat for a Hungarian refugee who'd first set foot in Sydney in 1949. He'd survived a Nazi death camp during the Second World War, and later a communist crackdown on Jews in his homeland. He'd managed to get out from behind the Iron Curtain to seek salvation and a new life in Australia. Abeles had started his own trucking business – Alltrans in 1951 – with just two second-hand lorries. By 1967 he was running a fleet of 500 wagons across Australia and had merged with Ken Thomas's Thomas National Transport – TNT. He was appointed Managing Director of TNT the following year. If ever a man deserved respect for scrapping his way to the top, Emil Herbert Peter Abeles did.

On our second day in Oz, Gina and I were invited over to Sir Peter's for what the rest of the world believe to be Australia's favourite pastime – a 'barbie' – but this was no ordinary barbeque. The weather wasn't playing fair, so Sir Peter moved his guests out of the rain and into the cellar of his palatial home. When you consider there were 200 guests, you begin to appreciate the humongous size of his cellar. Rain can sometimes put paid to cricket – another favourite Aussie pursuit – but it sure as hell wasn't putting out the flames on Sir Peter's BBQ.

The following day, Sir Peter's secretary, a lovely lady called Joy Finlay, invited us to her home for another barbeque, albeit one not so grand as her boss's. In the course of the evening she asked me where Gina and I would like to spend a week after the board meeting.

'How do you mean?' I asked.

'Well, you tell us where you'd like to go for a break with Gina and we can arrange it for you,' said Joy.

I didn't really know what to say. I hadn't expected the question. 'It'd be nice to go somewhere famous, something we can talk about to our friends and family when we get back home.' I was thinking maybe a few days on Bondi Beach. When we returned to our hotel there was an envelope on the pillow of the bed. This was intriguing. Inside were tickets for a flight up to Alice Springs, hotel reservations and then another pair of tickets for a flight onto the Uluru Nature Reserve – we were going up to Ayers Rock – one of the Great Natural Wonders of the World. Gina was ecstatic. I was pretty bloody happy as well.

The AGM came and went and the TNT delegates flew back to their respective businesses scattered around the world. Gina and I were off to see what the locals called 'Alice'.

It was like nowhere we'd ever been before. Alice Springs is situated roughly in the centre of Australia in the Northern Territory. It resembled what I'd call a 'cowboy town' – the sort of place you'd see in Western films – with lots of sidewalks, except the likes of John Wayne, Clint Eastwood and other movie characters never stepped out of the heat into an air-conditioned shopping mall.

When we went 'walkabout' we'd see the local Aborigines lying drunk on the banks of the Todd River – a river that hardly ever flowed in this extremely arid part of Oz. We'd had a chauffeur-driven car collect us at the airport and take us to this swish hotel – a hotel which specialised in nouveau cuisine. I scanned the menu for the evening meal. It was pretty fancy food, which wasn't a problem in itself, but I fancied something in addition to what was on offer. I asked the waiter, 'I couldn't have a plate of chips, could I?'

His answer was clear and typically direct by Aussie standards, 'If you want chips, mate, you'll find the shop 500 miles that way,' he said, pointing across the restaurant. I'd had my chips, so to speak!

The next day we flew up to Uluru. The highlight of the trip would be watching the sunrise over Ayers Rock – the 348-metre-high monolith – one of Australia's main tourist attractions. It's the sort of thing that *does* make you want to get out of bed in the morning. The rays of the sun turned the giant slab from ochre, to burnished orange and finally intense red. It was a sight to behold. I'd hired a Land Cruiser 4x4 vehicle, and we spent the day driving around the Olgas – a group of huge domed rock formations – in the remote and rugged terrain of the Uluru-Kata Tjuta National Park. It's an area considered sacred to the Aborigines. It all made for an eventful but tiring day. We returned to the hotel. A good night's sleep would be very welcome.

That soon changed as the phone clattered into life at 5am. What the hell?

'Where are you?' It was The Jones.

Bleary-eyed and still coming to my senses, I replied, 'Ayers Rock.'

'Where's that?'

'Bloody Australia, where do you think it is? Anyway, where are you?' I asked.

'Watford Gap Services. I want to go through some numbers with you,' and with that Alan started reeling off the figures of the Saturday night print run at Wapping. So there I was, stark bollock naked, on the floor, with a hotel pencil and pad from the bedside table, jotting down this barrage of numbers.

'How do they look to you?' asked Alan.

'Yes, they're about right.'

'I've got the delivery times. Write these down.' Alan fired off another battery of figures.

'They're alright, they're running to schedule, don't worry about it, the job's going fine,' I said reassuringly.

'Great, great. It's been good talking to you.' He rang off. It was another example of Alan's one-dimensional focus on the business. Ring a bloke on the other side of the world at the crack of dawn, no small talk, straight into the numbers and then curtail the call. At least somebody was looking after News International in my absence.

My first experience of Australia had been wonderful. It was a friendly place, very much a masculine environment, and it suited me down to the ground. I didn't know it at the time, but I'd be returning every year for the next 12 years on TNT business.

I say business, but there was always an element of pleasure on each trip, usually associated with horse racing and Ross Cribb. As well as being Sir Peter's 'First Lieutenant', he was also an aficionado of The Sport of Kings and owned a stud farm. What Ross didn't know about horse racing could be written on the back of a postage stamp. The TNT AGM was always held in November, sometimes clashing with Australia's most prestigious thoroughbred horse race – The Melbourne Cup, held on the first Tuesday in November every year. It's known locally as 'the race that stops a nation' because the vast majority of the country grinds to a halt to watch the 3,200-metre race. A crowd of 110,000 descends on Flemington Park Racecourse for the race, whereas the rest of the country tunes in on TV.

One year, David Mortimer, the new Managing Director who'd succeeded Sir Peter, had scheduled an AGM 'think tank' on Melbourne Cup day. It wasn't the best idea he'd ever had. We were attending a BBQ – naturally – at Mortimer's home on the night before the TNT cranial get-together, when Ross whispered to me, 'How do you fancy watching the Melbourne Cup?'

'I'd love to go, Ross, but I can't. David's running this think tank.'

'You leave that to me,' said Ross knowingly. 'Do you want to bring Atky along with you?'

'Yeah, he'd love it,' I said. Ross explained that he'd be taking us to Randwick Racecourse in the eastern suburbs of Sydney, where there'd be a big screen showing the race and on-site bookmakers – the next best thing to actually flying over to Melbourne. Mortimer had agreed to us effectively getting a free pass, and we had a wonderful day at the races.

The 'brainstorm' session duly went ahead without me and Atky, but it disintegrated when Bill Hanley was asked for his input. Mortimer turned to Bill and asked, 'What do you think, Bill?'

Bill replied in his inimitable way, 'I think you've sent the best two brains to the fucking races!' That was it – think tank over.

Another time, Ross took me and Atky to the Rosehill Gardens Racecourse, where he had an executive box, over in western Sydney. It was an amazing experience being with him on a race day. People would greet him, shake his hand, ask him how he was doing – there was so much warmth and friendship directed his way, such was the esteem in which he was held in racing circles. On this day he looked down the race card – the runners and riders – and imparted his wisdom.

'Get on number three in the first race.' The horse romped home in first place.

'Get on number five in the second.' That was our second winner of the day.

'Get on number two in the third.' That was the hat-trick. Ross was on fire and we were taking the bookies to the cleaners.

Ross said he wasn't betting on the fourth race. Me and Atky were on a roll so we placed our bets. We lost. Same thing on the fifth race. Ross didn't bet. We had a flutter. We lost again.

By the sixth and final race Ross was back placing his bet. 'Get on number three.' Did it win? Of course it did. Christ, he knew his horses.

He liked lots of sport, including Rugby League. I was at another AGM when he pulled me to one side. 'I've a special job for you this afternoon. I want you to go next door. The rugby league international is on the TV, it's Australia against England. I want you to settle down with a few beers, watch the game and update me on the score every quarter of an hour.' I couldn't believe my luck.

The match got underway. I'd be having a cold beer and, at the 15-minute mark, I'd slip back into the AGM and hand Ross a piece of paper with the score line written on it. On the half hour I returned with the second update of the match and handed the slip of paper over to Ross. One of the TNT country managing directors was presenting at the time and he was talking about '… discount this and discount that…' I could see Sir Peter going progressively redder in the face. I thought he was about to explode. 'Discounts?' he said in a manner which was both stern and dismissive. I reckoned he shared my stance on discounts and allowed myself a wry smile. I sensed the unease in the room as many of the other country MDs shuffled with their notes and presentations. If they'd intended suggesting discounts before the meeting, they certainly weren't anymore. A couple of them glanced at me as I made my way out of the room and back to the beer and rugby. It was a look that said 'You lucky bastard!'

Ross would tell me how things had been for him and Sir Peter in the late 60s and 70s when they were building TNT into an international business. He said the whole of the two families would go to Sydney Airport to wave them off. It had been a different era, one where the menfolk were literally 'reaching for the skies' and conquering new business frontiers.

Whenever Ross and his wife Pam came over to the UK, he'd insist that I drove him around. He enjoyed my company and I enjoyed his. I'd take him to Spurs for the football, Twickenham for the rugby internationals, and he used to love a night out at Wimbledon watching the greyhound racing. I remember picking him up from Claridge's, and I saw him coming out of a public phone box just outside the hotel. I said, 'Ross, what are you doing? You've got a phone in your room in the hotel.'

He said, 'I know, but have you seen how much they charge you?' He was a cracking fella; he had money but he knew its worth. He'd worked bloody hard to get it and he wasn't about to throw it around like confetti at a wedding.

Years later, after I'd retired from TNT, Gina and I were holidaying in Sydney. We went to the Catalina Restaurant in Rose Bay with Ross and Pam, along with one of my former prodigies at TNT Express, Bob Black, then Managing Director of TNT Australia.

Ross was in his early 80s and I could tell he wasn't his old self. He was still sharp in places, but he had the onset of dementia. It was still lovely to see him and I was touched by the first thing he said to me, 'You've retired – are they looking after you?' It was Ross through and through. Here he was, not in the best of health, and all he wanted to know was, was I alright. What a smashing bloke, so considerate, so kind. He was a great motivator and a very astute businessman. I miss him.

As much as I loved Australia I turned down the chance to run TNT Australia. It happened on David Mortimer's watch at a time when the company was struggling with its domestic business. I'd be lying if I said I wasn't tempted – I was – but it wasn't right at the time. It's a decision I've never regretted.

I was in Australia with Atky to try and help turn the business around. They literally weren't making any money. We'd been sent down from the UK. We made presentations, shared our ideas, our vision on how a TNT business should operate to make it a success. We took all our marketing and sales materials and handed them over. It wasn't rocket science to us, but it was as if we'd been beamed down from another planet. As our musical backdrop we'd played 'Things Can Only Get Better', the theme the Labour Party had used in the 1997 General Election in the UK. It had seemed appropriate, but TNT Australia were light years behind the UK and Ireland. It was incredible. Maybe things could actually get worse!

Mortimer dispatched his man from Personnel, Dick Siberson, to see if I'd take on the job of reviving the Australian business. I knew the company was having a lot of trouble with the unions and, with my background, I would've been the man to take them on and win.

I said, 'The only way you'll get this business back on its feet is by turning Botany Bay red with union blood.'

It wasn't what Siberson wanted to hear. 'Oh, erm, erm, Tom,' he spluttered, 'you have to be very careful where the unions are concerned. We can't afford to antagonise them.'

Antagonise them? I wanted to tackle the buggers head on and smash them. 'Unless you're prepared to take the unions on, this business will never make money,' I reiterated.

Siberson visibly shuddered at my words.

Mortimer asked me to meet with him to discuss the job. He couldn't understand my reluctance. I said, 'David, I'll tell you what I told Dick. Unless you take the unions on, you won't crack it. I've spent enough time in Australia to know what's going on.'

'Look, Tom, let me get Dick to put a package together for you and then we'll talk again.' They kept chasing me.

I was staying at the Sheraton Mirage Hotel in Port Douglas – a three-hour flight away from Sydney. I was there with Gina and my kids, Scott and Amy, along with Atky, his wife and their daughter, Megan, on an all expenses paid business trip-cum-holiday. I'd never stayed in a hotel like it, either before or since. It was absolutely breathtaking. Surrounded by a man-made lido and opening up onto four miles of gorgeous white beach, this place was heaven on earth. I've stayed in some of the best hotels in the world, but nothing has ever topped this. When I checked in, the receptionist had queried the booking.

'How long will you be staying? It says you're here for a fortnight, but that can't be right.'

'Yes, that's right,' I said. 'We're here for the two weeks.'

'But our guests don't stay for a fortnight, it's normally three or four nights,' she said disbelievingly.

'No, we're doing the fortnight.'

The place was so incredibly expensive, people just didn't stay 14 nights, but we were.

A couple of days in, and Dick Siberson flew out to see me again.

'We really do need you to take charge of the business in Australia.'

'Yes, I know, Dick, but like I've said, certain things need to change.'

He played what he thought would be his master stroke. 'I've three envelopes for you. The first contains all the details of your salary. The second is a special payment from David Mortimer. The third relates to the bonus scheme.' He handed them to me.

I took them and handed them straight back.

'But you haven't even opened them,' said Dick.

'No, and I'm not going to open them until you get serious about the job. You haven't talked about the role, about the backing I'd get in tackling the union, what changes you want to see. All you've done is put three envelopes in front of me and tried to bribe me.'

This wasn't what he'd expected, not one bit. 'But what am I going to tell Mr Mortimer?'

'Just tell him I don't want the fucking job!'

Poor old Dick couldn't believe it but, to his credit, he didn't give up. 'Can I see you in the morning, when you've had time to sleep on it?'

'If you like. I'll be down for breakfast at 7.30am.'

Sure enough, the next morning Dick was waiting in the hotel restaurant. 'Morning Tom.'

'Good morning, Dick. Have you spoken to David about it?'

'No,' said Dick.

'Well, I'm sorry Dick, the answer's no. Leave it to me, I'll phone David and explain.'

I rang Mortimer in Sydney, thanked him for the offer (*not that I knew what it was as I'd never opened the envelopes*) and told him I'd decided to stay in the UK.

We finished off the holiday of a lifetime and flew back to England. I went to see 'The Jones' and told him I'd turned down the Aussie role and was staying to work with him in the UK.

'You've made the right decision, Tom. Have you seen the size of the fucking flies down there?'

I burst out laughing. I'd just made the biggest decision of my career, one that could've taken me to the other side of the world, and in Alan's thinking it'd all come down to the size of some 'fucking flies'.

16

Going Dutch

The Dutch are a pedantic race. They're like a dripping tap on a stone – drip, drip, drip, drip, drip – repetitive and irritating. They try to wear you down. They're monotonous and tedious. To compare their approach to Chinese water torture would be unfair. The process in which water is slowly dripped onto a person's forehead to drive them insane is known to be effective. The Dutch, invariably, are not. To describe their takeover of TNT as a culture shock would be a chronic understatement. Your typical Aussie exudes verve and vitality. The plodding pedants from The Netherlands were the polar opposite. It was a dark day when the Dutch postal and telecommunications company, KPN, concluded a friendly takeover of TNT in late 1996.

When news of the deal first broke I was in Germany with Bill Hanley. We were surprised. Our German hosts were horrified. We were in Dusseldorf, working on a range of new initiatives to increase TNT Germany's market share and revenue streams. That soon went out of the window. The entire German senior management team resigned. The sentiment was, 'There's no way we're working for the fucking Dutch.' It was unbelievable. They just did it there and then. These were tumultuous times. We were instructed to return to the UK and await instructions.

Within an obscenely short period, our new paymasters from Holland had either alienated or replaced a number of key personnel in TNT management teams across Europe. These were people who'd historically performed well and made good money in their respective domestic markets. It didn't make sense. In fairness, they'd left me and the UK alone for a couple of years. We were making shedloads of money. Even the Dutch knew better than to fix what wasn't even remotely broken.

In 1999 The Jones was rewarded for his outstanding work in TNT UK. He was appointed as Group Managing Director of TNT Express, presiding over the Express business on a worldwide scale. The natural line of succession saw me promoted to Alan's old job, that of Managing Director of UK & Ireland. I'm not one for false modesty, neither would I describe myself as arrogant, but I'd more than earned my newly elevated status. Not only had I been the driving force behind TNT Newsfast, I'd also inherited an underperforming domestic parcels operation and transformed it into a veritable cash cow. The UK & Ireland was *the* most profitable business unit in the whole of TNT. It still didn't stop the Dutch from trying to undermine me.

Whereas I was raking in the money with the domestic parcels, the international arm of the UK business was haemorrhaging cash at an alarming rate. I wasn't responsible for TNT International, that was the domain of Roger Corcoran – a 'Ten-Pound Pom' from Bristol – who'd emigrated to Australia. We had diametrically opposing business philosophies. We were cut from entirely different cloth. When the Dutch took the strategic decision to merge the national and international businesses in each country, it meant there could only be one boss – it was either me or Corcoran. Ad Scheepbouwer, the Chairman and Chief Executive Officer of TNT's parent company, TPG, wanted Corcoran for the role. What a cheek. What an insult. What a joke. After everything I'd achieved they wanted to hand it all over to a guy who presided over failure.

The Jones went up against Scheepbouwer, insisting I was the

only man for the job. I'd been the brains behind TNT Express. I was the one posting year-on-year record-breaking profits, not Corcoran. My results spoke volumes, but even then I always got the impression the Dutch would've liked more of a 'yes man' in charge of the UK. I was a maverick. As it was, Alan's influence and my undoubted abilities and track record won the day. I took over TNT International in the UK, and what a bloody mess it was. I made it my job to visit all the International depots in the country. I wanted to see, first hand, what was required.

I went down to Bristol and spoke to this guy driving a forklift truck. He didn't know who I was. I said, 'Where's your Traffic Operator?' He replied, 'I'm the Traffic Operator.'

'Well, why are you driving a forklift?'

'Because I haven't got a forklift driver.' Fair enough, I thought.

I continued, 'What's the management structure in the depot?'

'You're looking at it! Me.'

This was ridiculous. 'Well, who orders the toilet rolls?'

'The next person who needs a shit,' came the retort from the man, who appeared to be all of Bristol depot rolled into one.

If that wasn't bad enough I was left gobsmacked and thirsty at our Worcester depot. The General Manager's secretary said apologetically, 'I'd make you a cup of coffee, Tom, but I can't. We don't have a kettle.'

I said, 'Why haven't you got a kettle?'

'We've been told by Roger that we can't afford one.' I got my wallet out and gave her a £20 note. 'Pop out and get the depot a kettle!'

No wonder morale was at rock bottom. The whole ethos was one of cost cutting, nit picking and negativity. There was no spark, no drive. The get up and go had got up and gone. It was bad. The whole business was floundering under a mountain of discount-related invoice queries – that sounded familiar! New blood was required. I 'imported' another of my prodigies – Stuart Stobie – all the way back from South Africa. Stobie had done well for me as a young General Manager at Maidstone, but he'd had ambitions to work overseas. I'd facilitated his move to Johannesburg. We applied the same blueprint, logic, principles and processes that had been instrumental in making TNT Express such a winner. The formula worked. Together we turned the international business from a loss-maker to a money-maker. Call it self confidence – not arrogance – but I had the Midas touch. I knew it, and the likes of Scheepbouwer knew it. It didn't make me untouchable, but not far off it.

When I was made MD of the UK & Ireland business, I remember thinking I would have to do something – something that had never been done before – to really make my mark. The Jones had won the European Quality Award and a couple of European Quality Prizes. I needed something that shouted, *'Tom Bell was here!'* I decided to go for a Queen's Award for Enterprise, arguably the highest accolade available, awarded for, 'Outstanding achievement by UK businesses…' We won it at the first attempt in the year 2000 under the 'Innovation' category. It was a huge feather in my cap and it resonated with the Dutch. They might not have liked me, but they couldn't deny me the credit I was due for earning the company such prestigious recognition.

I'll admit, I used to enjoy getting up their noses with some of my ways. If a bunch of soulless bureaucrats told me to do one thing, there was a good chance I'd do the opposite. I was supposed to file my financials – the budgets and accounts – in Euros. In all my time as MD I never did. It drove the buggers crazy, but I always got away with it. I remember attending a board meeting in Hoofddorp, near Amsterdam – the home of TNT's global headquarters. The assembled MDs from the various countries were asked how much profit they'd made the previous week. The replies from around the room revealed everybody was having a tough time hitting their targets. It was my turn to answer. 'We cleared three million.' They sought clarification, 'What? €3million?'

This was the moment. 'No. £3 million. Real money.' I could see the antagonism etched into their faces. It really pissed them off, but what wasn't there to like? They should've been smiling. £3 million was a better result than €3 million.

Scheepbouwer didn't stick around for too long. He went back to KPN. His replacement – Peter Bakker – stepped up from his role as Chief Finance Officer to CEO. Bakker was very keen on environmental matters, sustainability and all manner of green issues. He was a great guy to sit down with and share a few beers, a good guy. I got on alright with him. The only problem was, he knew bugger all about how to run a parcels business. On one visit to the UK I invited him to come along to the Atherstone hub to see how we did things. He declined the invitation, saying, 'There's no point.'

I said, 'What do you mean, there's no point?'

'I can't add anything. I wouldn't be able to add any value.'

I thought it was a really strange thing to say. We had a Chief Executive Officer who 'couldn't add any value'! I thought, *Well, what the hell are you supposed to be doing?*

He took me by surprise once during a private one-to-one conversation. He looked me in the eyes and said, 'You call me a twat, don't you?' I went straight back at him, 'No. I call you a fucking twat!' He just smiled. For a Dutchman, he had quite a well developed sense of humour. He certainly seemed to understand irony, something that is often lost on foreigners. I suppose you could say we had a love-hate relationship, but we made it work. He was likeable enough, and I certainly respected his passion for doing what he believed was right, especially his philanthropic work with the United Nations' World Food Programme.

I'll always be thankful to him for sending me to Cambodia, on what was a real eye-opener of a trip. TNT supported the WFP to the tune of £7.5 million each year. The company would send employees out on the front line, to witness how that money was used to literally save lives. Cambodia was a world removed from anything I'd ever experienced. We were funding a new irrigation system for paddy fields. Once installed and operational, it would enable the growing of three crops of rice each year instead of two.

It would make the people in the region self-sufficient for food. The project was very labour intensive. Entire families – mums, dads, the kids, even the grandparents – would be digging ditches, often with their bare hands. For each ton of earth dug out, the family would be given a tin of fish oil and a sack of rice. It was incredible to see the amount of effort that went in to gain, what we might view as, such a meagre reward. It reminded me of times gone by, when a family from a different generation would go out onto the sands of East Scotland, gathering their one and only source of fuel with their bare hands. I'd come a long way from the days of collecting sea coal, but it would never do to forget my roots and how tough life once was for me, and still was for others less fortunate.

Next up was a visit to a WFP-funded centre for sufferers of AIDS. We had to drive north from the capital Phnom Penh, with an overnight stop en route. The 'hotel' (*I use the term in the loosest sense*) was like nothing I'd ever seen before. It made my childhood tenement home in Kirkcaldy seem almost attractive. A strip of filthy flex hung from the ceiling with a dimly lit bulb on the end. The room was dirty. The bathroom was even dirtier, and to cap it all there was no toilet roll. The Sheraton Mirage Hotel in Port Douglas, it most definitely was not. I went down to the reception to ask for some toilet roll. Could I make them understand me? It was a bloody nightmare. The hotel didn't have a restaurant – which was probably a blessing – but I could go to a cafe, just across the road. The cost of the meal would be added to my hotel bill. The cafe was accessible, but only by crossing a four-lane road, with a thousand mopeds and motorbikes going past every minute. I chanced it and made it. I wish I hadn't bothered. The food was disgusting and completely inedible.

Instead, I made do with a few beers, sitting on the hotel steps watching the chaos of a Cambodian rush hour, one that seemed never-ending. The following morning I chanced the cafe for breakfast. I was starving. Once again the food was rank. Fuck it. I went into the kitchen, grabbed some eggs and made myself an omelette. By the time I'd finished and was ready to risk life and limb getting back to the hotel, the cheeky buggers had added omelette to their menu. It may even have been the Chef's Special.

We resumed our journey – and a bloody uncomfortable one at that – along bumpy tracks in the oppressive heat and humidity up to Siem Reap, the capital city of Siem Reap Province and a gateway to the Angkor region.

It's an increasingly popular tourist attraction. Our destination was as far removed from enjoying a holiday as it could get. We were heading for a hospice for those dying from AIDS. It was run by a local priest who'd just taken delivery of some new kit for cremating the poor souls who'd succumbed to the disease.

He was obviously a very compassionate man to even be doing the work he was doing, but he was highly enthused with his new gadget. It struck me as being rather macabre. He explained, via our WFP interpreter, that sudden and heavy rainfall would often extinguish the burning of dead bodies, causing all manner of hazards at the hospice. At least with the new machine, the cremation process could be carried out unhindered.

We went inside the hospice. I'll never forget a guy lying in a bed. He was wearing some kind of nappy. He was as weak as hell. Somehow he summoned up the strength to give me the traditional Cambodian greeting with hands clasped and a bow. I'll admit, it was a profoundly touching moment. He weighed less than my travel bag. He was riddled with disease and yet so dignified. He died four days later. It was the first time I'd ever met anybody with AIDS. I was truly humbled. It's something that will stay with me until my dying day.

A year after I'd retired, Bakker left TNT to become President and CEO of the World Business Council for Sustainable Development. It'd be right up his street. I bet he's never uttered the words, 'I can't add any value,' in that job. I've no doubt he'll be making his mark, and good luck to him.

Fair to say, we live in an age where we are bombarded with requests for charitable donations. We see literally dozens of TV adverts appealing for money every day. We're told that, 'For just £3 a month…' we can make a difference.

There are so many deserving causes competing for our money – where do we start? I made a choice back in 1997. I became aware of the Wooden Spoon, a wonderful little charity making a world of difference to the lives of children who were disadvantaged, either mentally or physically.

I was good at making money for TNT. What was to stop me generating much-needed funds to help improve the quality of life for tens of thousands of youngsters? 13 years and £3 million later I had the answer – nothing was going to stop me in my quest.

17

Changing lives

I'd watched the devoted dad as he reached inside the car. Carefully, slowly and expertly, he manoeuvred the young boy out of the vehicle and into the waiting wheelchair. It must've taken him the best part of 20 minutes since he'd parked up, but now he was on the move, taking his son to enjoy the highlight of the little lad's week. I was at a Riding for the Disabled project in Chessington, to see how TNT's funding for the Wooden Spoon was being put to best use.

With the help of our donations, the 'Spoon' had funded the building of an indoor riding arena. It meant that, come rain or shine, the disadvantaged youngsters would still be able to enjoy the thrill and sensation of riding a horse.

I went inside. The little boy I'd seen in his wheelchair was now on horseback, being led around the perimeter of the ring. His beaming smile would've warmed the coldest of hearts. He was gloriously happy. I went over to see him and the female riding expert leading the beautiful tan-coloured horse. 'Hello, what are you looking so happy about?' I asked in light-hearted fashion. The boy, who was probably eight or nine years old, said, 'This is the day that I get to ride a horse.'

'What's so special about riding a horse?' I asked, in the way you do when seeking a simple answer from a child.

'That's easy,' said the lad. 'This is the one day of the week when I can look down at people. I spend the rest of the week having to look up at them from my wheelchair.'

I hadn't expected that. His words really hit home. Here was a kid who had his whole world, his outlook on life, transformed by something as simple as riding a horse for 45 minutes each week. You could see the pride, joy and self-belief in his face. I learned from the riding instructor that a horse's natural gait stimulated muscles that lie dormant in a child confined to a wheelchair. It was fascinating, enlightening and rewarding. This was why I was channelling TNT's best fundraising efforts towards the Spoon.

I first heard about what was then The Wooden Spoon Society at a golf tournament being hosted by one of my customers – Peter Nichol. He was the owner and Managing Director of Grange Packaging, a company which supplied hampers for TNT employees at Christmas. He'd invited me over to Hawkstone Park Golf Club in the spring of 1997. The day's golf had gone well and I was attending dinner in the evening. There must've been more than 50 people present and I was the odd one out. Everyone was wearing a strange tie comprising red, white, blue and green stripes. It certainly caught the eye – it was a bit on the 'loud' side. They were the colours of the four home nations, Wales, England, Scotland and Ireland. It was the tie of the Spoon – the charity of British rugby. After dinner a softly spoken Glaswegian, Gerry Brophy, stood up and gave a speech about 'Stirring Smiles', explaining the ethos of the Spoon and how it came about.

He really caught my attention when he said 96% of all monies raised went directly to frontline causes. There weren't many charities that had overheads of just 4%. I was impressed.

Gerry explained the origins of the Spoon and why it had the unlikeliest of names. It began in a pub in Dublin in 1983 after England had lost to Ireland 25-15. Some English fans were drowning their sorrows. The Irish had beaten them, and their country had finished rock bottom of the Five Nations Championship (France making up the five). Triumphant and in high spirits (more likely, Guinness) some Irish supporters presented the vanquished English with a symbolic consolation prize – a wooden spoon. On their flight back to London, the England supporters spotted Irish and British Lions rugby legend Willie John McBride and asked him to sign the spoon.

They subsequently arranged a charity golf day to see who would 'retain' the wooden spoon. The event raised £8,450 – enough to buy a minibus for a special needs school. The fundraising events continued and registered charity status followed.

I invited Gerry to the TNT annual golf day at The Belfry in July 1997. He delivered the same speech to an audience of 200 and we collected £10,000 on the night. I phoned the Spoon headquarters the next day and asked where to send the donation. I was surprised to be told they didn't want the £10k. Instead they preferred bricks.

'We'd like it if you could phone the London Brick Company, order £10k's worth of bricks and have them delivered to the Birmingham Children's Hospital. We're building a cancer unit for the treatment of teenagers. If you order them, the invoice will go to you at TNT and we won't have any admin work. 100% of the money will go directly towards the unit,' said the Spoon lady. So, that's what I did.

Not only did they keep overheads to a minimum, they only funded capital projects, tangible stuff such as buildings, sensory rooms and play areas. They didn't fritter it away on 'airy fairy' things.

I've always believed that if a job's worth doing, it's worth doing properly. If TNT was going to make a serious and sustainable financial contribution to the Spoon, we needed to draw on the company's competitive DNA. I introduced league tables across the depots, the regions and the business divisions to see who could raise the most money. It worked a treat, and the donations sky-rocketed. 1998 saw a trebling of our initial donation to £30k. Within nine years that annual figure increased tenfold. We smashed the £300k barrier in 2007 and went on to hit £305,137 in 2010, the year I retired. In total, the TNT employees, supported by our customers and suppliers, raised in excess of £3 million in 12 years during my time at the helm. We were by far and away the biggest single contributor to the Spoon.

A year after bringing the Spoon to my attention, Peter Nichol invited me back to his golf day at Hawkstone Park. Little did I know that it was the onset of years of playing practical jokes on each other, with the Spoon always coming out smiling, courtesy of ever-increasing donations.

I arrived at the splendid Shropshire course in plenty of time for the early morning coffee and bacon sandwiches. The player pairings for the day were drawn at random, with the names of professionals, semi pros, celebrities and amateurs coming out of a hat. As the draw drew to a conclusion, all the two-man teams seemed well matched with a more than capable golfer – someone who could hit the ball 250+ yards off the tee – in each pairing. My name had yet to be called. I was casting an eye around the clubhouse, but my playing partner – whoever it was – was nowhere in sight. At this point I felt a tapping on my knee. I looked down.

'Hi, I'm Kenny Baker, your playing partner for the day.' A dwarf was looking up at me, offering his outstretched hand. I was caught off guard. I'll admit, I was momentarily bemused as we shook hands.

'You probably don't recognise me, but I play R2D2 in the *Star Wars* movies – you know, the little robot character – Luke Skywalker's mate.'

I didn't want to appear rude, but discovering my playing partner was only 3' 8" tall wasn't what I'd expected. 'Morning, pleased to meet you.' I heard the words coming out of my mouth, but I couldn't hide my shock. 'You don't play, do you?' It wasn't a question designed to cause offence, but I was still trying to get my head round what was going on.

'Yeah, I play,' said Kenny, 'but I'm a bit worried about going in the buggy. I prefer to walk and carry my golf bag.'

We went outside and there was Kenny's bag – it was huge and must've been 2ft higher than him. This was getting more bizarre by the second. We made our way to the driving range to practise before teeing off. Kenny was dragging this bag along the ground. My instincts were to offer to help, but he seemed happy with the situation. I didn't want to patronise him.

'Are you going to hit a few balls?' I asked.

'No, I won't bother wasting my energy. Anyway, you be careful with your swing, I hear you've had a bad back. How's it feeling?' I thought, *That's a bit weird, how does he know I've had a bad back?* I hit a couple of practice shots and then it was time for us to tee off. Despite his earlier concerns about riding in a golf buggy, Kenny got in. He sat down with his feet in the air; obviously he couldn't reach the floor. He gripped the seat to ensure he didn't fall out.

We were called to the first tee, but instead of Kenny stepping forward this strapping six-foot golf professional walked up to my side and shook my hand. 'I'm your playing partner for the day.' I thought, *What the hell is going on?* All of a sudden I could hear Nichol. He was nigh on delirious, pissing himself with laughter. He'd set me up and I'd fallen for it hook, line and sinker. Everybody was in hysterics, including Kenny. The story had it that when Peter hired Kenny he asked his agent, 'How will I recognise him? The agent had replied, 'Well, he's 3' 8" tall – what do you want him to do – wear a pink carnation in his buttonhole?'

Peter is reputed to have replied, 'Yes, I think that would be helpful.' It would be typical Nichol – a smashing bloke with a real sense of fun. As ever it was a great day and the money flowed in for the Spoon. As soon as the night was over I began plotting my revenge for 1999.

12 months on and it was my turn to have a laugh at Nichol's expense. With Hawkstone Park's permission I booked a comedy

troupe, the 'Wacky Waiters'. The actors and actresses would blend in with the staff and appear to be normal workers.

Nichol always prided himself on producing a slick event. As we prepared for dinner, he wasn't best pleased to see this bloke cleaning the interior windows of the restaurant. He mumbled something to me about it 'not being acceptable', but he didn't make a fuss. Next up, an electrician arrived and made his way over to our table.

Thrusting a pair of stepladders into Nichol's hands, the pseudo sparky said, 'Here you go, mate, just hold these!' Peter's face was a picture. The electrician crawled under the table, disappeared from sight and drilling noises ensued for a minute or so. Nichol stormed off, looking for Hawkstone Park's General Manager.

The GM, who was in on the joke, made sure he couldn't be contacted. By the time Peter returned the electrician had gone. He'd calmed down, and we sat down at the table. Act three came in the shape of the wine waiter. Convention dictates the waiter uncorks the bottle and pours a sample for the head of the table to taste. Once approved, the waiter then pours wine for all the other diners. My wacky waiter uncorked the wine, took a swig from the bottle and said, 'Yeah, that's fine, that'll do you,' before placing the bottle down and walking off.

I could see Peter was far from happy but trying to keep his cool. Next thing, the soup course arrived. The waiter had a big bandage around his thumb, and his thumb was immersed in Nichol's soup. Peter was clearly exasperated but equally reluctant to make a scene. It took a waitress wearing gauntlet gloves and carrying a bucket to finally tip him over the edge. Rather than taking the plates away at the end of the main course, she made a big show of plonking the bucket on the table and scraping any leftover food into it. This was too much for Nichol. He was just about to lose it when I leaned over and said, 'That's what you get if you play with fire, you little shit! You got me with the dwarf, so it's my turn this year!'

He burst out laughing. 'You bastard, you've done me, and at my own golf day!' I would have been prepared to leave it at that, but not

Nichol. Whereas I was happy having had him back for his jolly jape, Peter wanted to take it up a notch or two.

I was presenting prizes at The Belfry on TNT's golf day alongside our guest of honour, former World Heavyweight Boxing Champion, Frank Bruno, when all hell broke loose. Up to a dozen dwarfs invaded the stage and handcuffed me to Bruno. Poor old Frank – 6' 3" tall and 18 stone of sheer muscle – was totally bemused. He had a look of blind panic as the dwarfs slapped the cuffs on us. I hadn't a clue what was happening – and then the penny dropped.

It was dwarfs again, so it must be Nichol. The audience cheered as Peter stepped up with keys to the handcuffs. By now Bruno was laughing his distinctive 'baritone' laugh and the place just dissolved into stitches.

Once again the Spoon laughed all the way to the bank, with £165,000 raised – a good hike on the previous year's total of £103,000. Another example of our battle of the pranks came when I sabotaged Nichol's golf dinner by installing airport-like security scanners at Hawkstone Park. Once again, the golf course management played along. The ladies had to remove their shoes and have their handbags checked, whereas the men were required to take off their jackets, belts and shoes. I had up to 120 people queuing to go into the restaurant and Nichol was going nuts.

Peter embodied the spirit of the Spoon. He worked hard and he played hard. He grafted and he partied. The essence of Spoon fundraising was speculate to accumulate. It was a winning formula.

It was an approach shared by Geoff Morris, who joined the Spoon as the new Chief Executive in 2001. We hit it off immediately. He was innovative and keen to forge even stronger ties with TNT. He took it upon himself to visit all of our depots and, in 2003, together we launched 'Seeing is Believing' – an initiative to encourage thousands of TNT employees to engage directly with disadvantaged kids. Our people were raising hundreds of thousands of pounds for the Spoon, and Geoff wanted them to witness, first hand, how the money was being used. We'd give them paid time off work to visit Spoon-sponsored projects and interact with the youngsters. They would return to the depots and offices as ambassadors.

Who could fail to be touched and inspired by seeing children overcoming the hurdles of being disadvantaged mentally, physically and, more latterly, socially?

I certainly wasn't immune from the raw emotions that came so easily on a Seeing is Believing visit. I was at the Tiny Tim Centre in Coventry, a facility that offered a range of therapies for children, where treatment is either limited or not available on the NHS, or is not affordable to families from the private sector.

I'll never forget one conversation I had with the mother of two youngsters with autism. The mum said, 'I can't thank you enough for what you're doing.'

'There's no need to thank me, it's a privilege. If there's anything we can do to help the children, we'll try and do it.'

I wasn't expecting what came next.

'I'm not thanking you for what you do for my children, I'm thanking you for what you do for me. I have two autistic boys and the two days a week they come here are *my* two days. I spend the first day cleaning the house, going to the supermarket and doing the chores – all the things I don't get the chance to do when I'm looking after the kids.

'The second day is *my* day. I might go and get my hair done, meet friends for a coffee or go out to lunch and then maybe do some window shopping or even treat myself to a little something. It's my *me time* – without it I'd go absolutely mad. I love my kids so much, but if it was just me looking after them 24/7/365 it would drive me insane.' It was humbling and hugely gratifying to be able to help make that difference. It put into perspective how relatively simple gestures and acts of kindness can have such a positive and profound impact on people's lives.

As the recognised charity of the four home rugby nations, there never was, and never will be, a shortage of high-profile players and ex-players, more than willing to do their bit. I've had the pleasure of mixing with some of the giants of the sport in our collective support for the Spoon. Willie John McBride – the man who signed the original wooden spoon on the flight from Dublin to London back in 1983 – is a national treasure across the Irish Sea, something very evident when we spent an afternoon visiting a play centre for disabled children in Ireland. What a wonderful, warm and compassionate man.

The next day I was in Wales with one of Welsh rugby's favourite sons, Sir Gareth Edwards. Spoon had broadened its criteria to include socially disadvantaged children and I was there to see the stunning results. A painting project with the Cardiff Blues rugby club had altered the lives of a bunch of teenagers who were heading for a life of trouble, crime and probably jail time. They'd participated in a project to capture their rugby heroes on canvas, with the best paintings being displayed inside the Blues' ground. The project had given them a sense of purpose and achievement, re-establishing their self-esteem and levels of self-belief. It had made a difference.

I spent many hours with England's 2003 World Cup winning skipper Martin Johnson – a great bear of a man – who was a marvellous ambassador for the Spoon. He played for Leicester Tigers – just down the road from TNT's headquarters at Atherstone – and, as such, he was very generous with his time. TNT commissioned the making of a 5ft-long wooden spoon – an ideal prop for photo calls and media opportunities. It was solid wood and pretty heavy. I'll always remember 'Johno' playing in a ball pit with some of the children and a press photographer asking him to lift up one of the kids for a photo.

Johno – all 6' 7" and nearly 19 stone – popped a three-year-old girl on the end of the oversized spoon, lifted her up to shoulder level at an angle of 90 degrees, with just the one arm. Talk about strong! As a Scotsman I certainly didn't envy my fellow countrymen who had to do battle with the English colossus out on the rugby pitch.

Not only did Spoon enjoy the support of the UK's rugby fraternity, it also had a very special patron – none other than The Princess Royal, Princess Anne. Throughout my career with TNT there would be numerous occasions when I would meet members of the Royal Family. I was living in Burton Hastings, a village just outside Nuneaton, when I was first invited to meet Princess Anne. Gina and I were due to attend a Spoon-related lunch at Buckingham Palace and word had gone round the village. Ray Jones, the local blacksmith, saw me a couple of days before the event and said, 'Give my regards to Anne when you see her.' I thought he was on a wind-up. 'You know her, then, do you?'

'Oh yes. I do blacksmith demonstrations every year at the Gatcombe Horse Trials. Anne rides out every morning and I cook a bacon and egg roll over the coals for her breakfast.'

The lunch was held in the Chinese Room at Buck House. I was sitting to the right of the Princess, Gina was on her left. We'd been getting along famously talking about TNT's fundraising, the Spoon and rugby (The Princess Royal is Patron of the Scottish Rugby Union) and I thought, should I mention Ray? Will I make a fool of myself?

'By the way, ma'am, Ray Jones, the blacksmith, sends his best regards.'

'Oh, you know Ray, do you? Please say hello to him on my behalf.' What a relief – Ray did know her after all.

At that point the lunch arrived. The food came around on a tray and you helped yourself. You'd pour soup from a jug for starters and take a couple of slices of meat and vegetables for the main. The dessert was a strawberry tart, so you're expected to take a slice and pass the tray to the person sitting to your right. The Princess would go first, I was second and, because Gina was sitting to Princess Anne's left, she'd be last. When the dessert tray reached Gina all the tart had gone.

The Princess was aghast. 'This house doesn't run out of food. Whatever is going on?' Anne turned to Gina and proffered her slice of strawberry tart, 'Have mine.'

Gina, ever mindful of the etiquette of the occasion, replied, 'No, ma'am. Thank you, but I couldn't.'

Anne insisted, 'Please take it. I have another function to attend later tonight; I could do without it.' Gina had the Royal dessert. I'd never seen so many Palace flunkies in a tiswas over a tart. What had happened? Who was to blame? Had they served enough portions? Had some greedy bugger taken two slices? The Princess Royal had conducted herself as you'd expect, in exemplary style. I'm not so sure her father, Prince Philip, would've been quite so forgiving.

I've spent more time in the Duke of Edinburgh's company than any other member of the Royal Family. He doesn't suffer fools gladly; in fact, he doesn't suffer fools at all. His public image is that of a straight talker, a man who shoots from the hip, with political correctness more often than not in the crosshairs. I have to say I found him to be a great conversationalist, quick-witted and a man passionate about the awards scheme that bears his name.

The Duke of Edinburgh's Award (DofE) is a programme which recognises adolescents and young adults for completing a series of self-improvement exercises. Prince Philip began it all in 1956. Since then, eight million youngsters have taken on the challenge in more than 140 countries.

The objectives of the DofE sat well with TNT's ethos of striving for continual improvement. We shared a common philosophy. We were a good match. TNT were willing and able supporters. Over a period of time Prince Philip and I were no strangers to each other.

Whenever TNT hosted a major DofE event it would invariably fall to me to deliver a speech, to which the Duke would reply. I've done so in historic locations all over Britain. One of the most memorable was a banquet for 200 guests at Edinburgh Castle on a beautiful summer evening. As was always the case, we were briefed about the Duke's schedule. On this occasion he would depart at 22.30 hours on the dot. Sure enough, Prince Philip rose to leave at bang on 10.30pm, but instead of departing the venue he invited me to accompany him. I was intrigued. In the courtyard outside were two thrones – one for the Duke and one for me. We heard the skirl of the pipes from the Castle's ground. It was getting louder and louder. The pipers were marching up to the courtyard. Within a couple of minutes they were with us, accompanied by some female Highland dancers. This was an unexpected delight and a great way to conclude proceedings. An hour later Prince Philip bade me farewell, saying how much he'd enjoyed the evening.

Our next meeting was nowhere near as grand, as the Duke wrong-footed Special Branch and hardly said a word to me. I was at the Royal Windsor Horse Show presenting a new 40ft trailer to the DofE from TNT. It featured climbing walls, computer equipment and a host of other activities to help encourage kids to sign up for the Award. An officer from Special Branch had briefed me, telling me the Duke would come down from my right, greet me and then inspect the trailer. No problem. So, what happened? The Duke appeared from between a burger van and a chip van from my left-hand side, devoid of any security detail.

'Ah, it's you again,' said Prince Philip.

'Yes, sir,' I replied.

'Where's the driver of this thing? I want to speak with him,' said HRH.

I located the man who'd be taking the trailer all around the country in the days, weeks, months and years that lay ahead. The Prince spent an hour with the driver, asking a whole host of questions, wanting to know every detail about the how, why, who, what and where of all aspects of the roadshow. He was very interested in how it would stimulate young minds and benefit the young Duke of Edinburgh students. Finally he'd finished with the driver. He shook his hand, turned to me and said, 'Cheerio.' Never one to stand on ceremony, he was gone.

Our next encounter also had members of the Royal Protection Unit in a flap. I was hosting another Duke of Edinburgh's Award dinner at Cardiff Castle. Gina and I were staying at the Hilton Hotel opposite the medieval structure. We'd arrived in casual mode

– jeans and T-shirts – checked in and were just about to go up to our room in the lift.

'Sir, madam, please move to one side.' We were being shepherded away to the side of the reception. There was a burst of activity at the hotel entrance and the Duke of Edinburgh was moving towards the lift with his police detail. As he reached the elevator he spotted me.

'Not you again,' he said with a big smile.

'Yes, sir, you've got me again. I'll see you over at the Castle.' The Special Branch boys heard the conversation and were looking at me, thinking, *Who the hell is this bloke?* The Duke went off in the lift. It was rather nice having Prince Philip recognise and greet me in such a fashion. We were chatting away later that evening. He leaned towards me, 'What do you think to the hotel?'

I said, 'It's very nice and especially handy for the Castle.' He then made me laugh.

'I got in the bath and there was no bloody soap. I had to get out and have someone go and get some.

'I'll have to have a word with Charles. He's got a castle or two around here; he must have one I can stay in. He is the Prince of Bloody Wales, when all is said and done.' I liked Prince Philip. We rubbed along well and we shared a common goal of wanting to see young people flourish and fulfil their potential. One of the greatest days of my life would be a 'date' with his wife, one that I will cherish forever.

18

Do you want a medal for it?

Instigating positive change in the life of any child is a cause for celebration. Helping those youngsters most in need in our society is a reward in itself. Shaping better and more fulfilling lives for tens of thousands of disadvantaged children is a privilege beyond compare. I've been incredibly fortunate in my time. I've had the power and influence to make all of these things happen, but I could never have done it on my own.

From the moment I first heard about the Wooden Spoon, I became a massive advocate. To me, Spoon was a hidden gem, a little diamond waiting for a chance to truly shine. Comparatively unknown outside of rugby union circles, it punched well above its weight in enriching the lives of mentally, physically, and later socially, disadvantaged kids. Mobilising the juggernaut-like support of TNT and throwing it behind the Spoon made perfect sense. As market leaders in the UK and Ireland's express delivery sector, we sure as hell weren't going to hang around when it came to raising millions of pounds in donations. The Spoon became the focal point of TNT's Corporate Social Responsibility activities. The adage that it is 'better to give than to receive' was never truer. The gargantuan efforts of TNT workers, their families, our suppliers and customers would have an enormous impact. The influx of funds would enable Spoon to do more than ever before for those they sought to help.

Sensory rooms and gardens, cancer treatment units and building works, playgrounds and play equipment, sports programmes and outdoor activities, education projects and investment in transportation – all needed funding. We weren't just there to raise money, we were also there to boost the Spoon's profile in the media and encourage others to support its work.

Unbeknown to me, somebody was busy raising my profile and my role in orchestrating the donations totalling £3 million. I only became aware when a very official looking envelope was delivered to my home one Saturday morning in November 2009. It was from Buckingham Palace. The Royal communiqué asked me a simple question – and I paraphrase, *'Would you be prepared to accept an OBE and become an Officer of the Most Excellent Order of the British Empire, for your services to charity?'*

It's not every day you open something like that over your tea and toast or coffee and cornflakes. I couldn't quite take in what I'd just read. I read it again, only this time out loud to Gina. She began to cry. My hands were shaking. It was a heady concoction of delight and almost disbelief. I was being offered an OBE in the Queen's New Year's Honours list of 2010. It began to sink in. Gina was still in tears. There was a reply slip to go back in another official looking envelope. I could either accept the honour or decline the OBE. Unlike David Bowie, LS Lowry, George Harrison, Nigella Lawson, Roald Dahl, Dawn French and Jennifer Saunders, to name but some, I wasn't about to refuse the honour. The adrenaline was still coursing through my veins, but I managed to write my response, pop it in the pre-paid envelope and get it in the post – and all within half an hour of receiving the Royal notification. Personal recognition wasn't something I'd ever sought or even dreamed about in my fundraising efforts. My focus had always been on doing the best we could to help the children and their families.

As Gina and I recovered from the shock – albeit a very pleasant one – we realised we had to adhere to the Royal protocols which accompany the awarding of an OBE. We were to tell no one about it. Instinctively, I wanted to ring my kids, my family and friends. The etiquette of the Honours' system dictated otherwise. It must not become public knowledge until it became official at one minute past midnight on New Year's Day 2010. I was bursting with pride, but it had to remain a secret. Keeping my mouth shut was going to be the hardest part, but we were sworn to secrecy. Neither Gina nor I were going to jeopardise it by breaking with convention. So much was going through my mind. This was one of the greatest moments in my life.

It dawned on me that I was going to be in esteemed company. The Jones was an OBE and Bill Hanley was an MBE – I was joining an elite club with the two most influential figures in my career. It was indeed an honour on so many levels. I wanted to pick up the phone and tell them. Of course I couldn't, but it got me thinking about the men to whom I owed so much.

Whereas I was being recognised for trying to enhance the lives of disadvantaged kids, I'd worked alongside a man who'd created countless opportunities for so many people. The Jones cut a charismatic figure. He could walk into any TNT depot and make anyone and everyone feel 10ft tall. I've never known an individual so driven by their work and yet so caring about the people within that workplace. He only ever saw the good in people, and if you worked for TNT you were one of 'his' people. He wanted to create a perfect work environment, one which would develop and reward excellence and maximise the potential of those willing to work to attain it.

It was Alan who insisted we pursued Investors In People (IIP) accreditation. I'd say, 'Why are we wasting our time on this? The staff already know they're well looked after.'

Alan was simple and spot on. 'Because we can help improve our people, both inside and outside the workplace. We should be doing things to give them the chance to be the best that they can possibly be. They develop new and existing skills, they enhance their levels of performance, they benefit, and we, as their employer, benefit.'

Taking Alan's lead, we formed a partnership with Nottingham University and created a two-year Management Degree programme. It opened educational doors to those who'd found them firmly closed in their youth. Under the IIP process, 25 TNT candidates per annum would now push at an open door and embrace exciting opportunities. It didn't matter if you worked on the loading bay, you were a driver, a customer adviser, a sales rep, an office worker or whatever, if you could pass the initial aptitude test you'd be given every consideration for a place on the programme. Obviously a candidate had to show they had the essential learning capacity. It wasn't in anybody's best interests if an individual would be out of their depth and destined to fail. Nor was it a wise investment. What it was from day one was a huge success.

The Jones was as meticulous as he was motivational. Not only could he see the 'bigger picture', he never overlooked any of the fine detail. When I wrote the 175-page proposal for Rupert Murdoch at Wapping in 1985, Alan insisted on scrutinising every word, every sentence and every paragraph. He would say to me, 'Tom, have you checked this?' I'd tell him I had. 'Yes, but have you double-checked?' would be his comeback line. I've never known a man more committed to excellence. He was incredible.

Working with The Jones was a real privilege, often an education, on a daily basis. We shared so many momentous moments and wonderful occasions. It was a very sad day for me when he finally decided he'd had enough of the Dutch pedants and all of the accompanying frustrations.

I made sure I was in Express House in Atherstone on The Jones' final day with TNT. It was the end of 2003 and I deliberately waited back until Alan was ready to leave. I wanted to walk out of the door with him one last time. We took the lift to the ground floor – just the two of us – not a word was spoken. We went into the reception. Alan said goodbye to the girls on reception – I think Julie, Denise and Sheila were on duty – I had a lump in my throat. We walked out onto the car park and shook hands. Still neither of us spoke. Words weren't required. The Jones went to his car and I went to mine. I got in and, I'm not ashamed to say, I shed a tear. It felt like a part of me had been cut away.

The other major influence on me at TNT was the guy I'd first spoken to way back in 1977, late on a Friday afternoon at the diesel pump in Maidstone depot. I'd asked, 'Who the fuck are you?' as he'd opened the passenger door to my Inter County Express truck. I got to know who Bill Hanley was soon enough, and my life was all the better for doing so. People used to say to me, 'Bill doesn't say a lot, does he?' They were right, he didn't, but when he did it was invariably profound. He was an astute man who knew the value and worth of everything in the business. He was 'old school' and I mean that as a compliment. If he was presented with a set of figures he'd always go through them – calculator at the ready – to ensure he understood and agreed with the numbers. It didn't matter if they'd come from the Finance Director or Chief Accountant. It was Bill's way and it served him well.

I worked very closely with Bill on the TNT Newsfast business. We forged a very strong bond. Rupert Murdoch would hold a senior management meeting first thing every Monday morning. It was a bit of a ball-breaker. Bill would come down to Heathrow on the first shuttle from Manchester and I'd collect him from the airport. We'd chat en route about how we were performing on the News International contracts and then present to Murdoch.

I recall being on another drive with Bill – down to London – when Bill had a chauffeur. The wily Lancastrian asked me, 'Do you want to stop at Toddington Hill Services for a sandwich or would you rather go to the Hilton Park Lane for lunch?' If that question was put to you, which one would you choose? Of course, you're going to say the Hilton – which I did.

'Oh, so the cafe at Toddington Services isn't good enough for you nowadays?' was Bill's reply. He had no intention of going to Toddington, neither was he being offensive. We'd both known what my reply would be. Nonetheless, if I'd been tempted to start getting too big for my boots, it was an effective way of bringing me back down to earth.

I once asked Bill why I'd been chosen for the TNT Newsfast position and entrusted with the crucial News International contract. 'I picked you, lad. You're no salesman, but you're a bloody good operator and you work hard.' Coming from Bill, that was high praise indeed. He wasn't one for giving out too many plaudits and compliments, so if and when you received one it would've been hard earned and well deserved.

He had a dry and disarming sense of humour, one that would often catch people when least expected. Bill and I would go on golfing breaks to France with some of the other guys from TNT and I remember him paying a compliment to Daniel Vines, one of our top sales managers at the time, and now Managing Director of Sales for FedEx in the UK. Bill was on his feet addressing the guests at the golf dinner. Daniel was seated a few feet away and Bill turned to him.

'You remind me of Brad Pitt's brother.'

Daniel was as pleased as punch. 'Cheers, Bill. I didn't know he had a brother.'

'Oh, he has. He's called 'Cess'!' The whole table burst into laughter.

Bill and Alan had both been honoured by the Queen in the same year, 1996, and here I was, 14 years later, emulating my mentors.

When I was first notified of the honour, I knew nothing other than it related to my work with the Spoon. Only later did I discover that Geoff Morris, Spoon's Chief Executive between 2001 and 2007, and David Walker, TNT's Head of Communications, had collaborated on the nomination, elicited a host of supporting endorsements and submitted it via the Cabinet Office. The process is such that an Honours Committee sits to decide which of the nominations should be approved. Their decision is passed through to the Prime Minister, who then conveys it to the Queen.

On January 1st, 2010, I was officially Tom Bell OBE. It was a tremendous feeling, a mixture of achievement, accompanied by an overriding sense of humility. Yes, I'd been the architect of TNT's relentless fundraising plans, but without the sterling efforts of thousands of men and women within the company, our suppliers and our customers, it could easily have fallen on stony ground. Yes, I'd be the one meeting the Queen and having the medal pinned on my jacket, but that medal belonged to everyone who selflessly channelled their time and energies helping disadvantaged children.

In military circles there's a joke that the letters OBE stand for *Other Buggers' Efforts*. I'd be the first to acknowledge that my OBE was the result of a sustained and tenacious approach not just by me, but by so many others. It just so happened I was the one required to attend a date with the Queen at Buckingham Palace.

Nearly six months later and the day finally dawned. It was Wednesday June 2nd and I was off to the Palace.

Over the years, I'd attended numerous lunches and events at Buck House, but this would be like no other. This was destined to be one of the greatest days in my life and I'd be sharing the moment with my loved ones – Gina, Scott and Amy. The investiture would take place in the Palace Ballroom, and my wife and kids would be there to witness Her Majesty The Queen pin the OBE medal on my chest. Upon arrival at the Palace the investees are given a quick brief as to what the ceremony entails. A special clip is attached to your jacket, to enable the medal to be presented swiftly and efficiently. Tradition has it that the Queen enters the Ballroom attended by the Queen's bodyguard – the Yeoman of the Guard. The National Anthem is played, and the military band continues to play a variety of music while the recipients of the honours are called forward, one by one, usually by the Lord Chamberlain.

In my case, I was to walk forward to a Royal Navy Commander who would 'release me' to approach the monarch as my citation was being read out. I was to walk forward until my toes touched the base of the dais, where the Queen was standing. The nerves kicked in. It wasn't rocket science. Just walk and stop at the dais. What could go wrong? I was still nervous. I took the few short steps and was immediately face to face with Her Majesty. As she fixed the OBE to my jacket she said, 'I believe my daughter has something to do with this charity?'

My turn to speak. 'Yes, ma'am, she's our patron.'

'And how much have you raised for the charity?'

'We've raised £3 million in 12 years, ma'am.'

'Well, please continue the good work,' said the Queen as she shook my hand.

I bowed, turned to the right and exited the presentation hall. The actual exchange with the Queen had taken three minutes, maybe four. The OBE and clip were removed from my jacket. The medal was laid in a presentation box and handed to me. I was then shown back into the hall to watch the rest of the ceremony. You're expected to observe a level of decorum in the hall, but once the investiture concludes you can fully enjoy the moment outside with your family, have photographs taken by the official Palace photographers and chat with the other investees. In my case I struck up a conversation with Formula One World Champion Jenson Button. He'd been made an MBE for his services to Motorsport, and yet there was me working in the superfast world of express deliveries, getting an OBE for my services to charity. He was a very personable bloke. The sun was shining, it was a beautiful summer's day and everything had gone like clockwork. It'd been a wonderful experience and it was now time to celebrate with family, friends, colleagues, and some of the people who'd helped me and TNT make such a worthy contribution to the Wooden Spoon.

We had a reception and lunch for 120 guests at the Landmark Hotel in Marylebone Road. I used the hotel as my base whenever I was in London on business, so it was an ideal choice when it came to mixing business with pleasure. Tracy Ford, my PA, had worked closely with the Landmark's manager, Douglas Glen, to ensure everything was spot on. As I arrived with Gina and the kids, I was greeted to a rousing chorus of 'For He's a Jolly Good Fellow,' and three 'Hip Hip Hoorays'. It was a nice way to start proceedings. I was especially pleased to see Geoff Morris and his wife Suzanne. They'd travelled down from Pittenweem – a fishing village in Fife and only 20 miles from my birthplace of Kirkcaldy – on the overnight sleeper train. It was gratifying that people were happy to make such an effort to be with me on such a special occasion.

Geoff had been a great Chief Exec at the Spoon. He'd fully bought into the essence of the charity – that of making heaps of money for great causes, but never losing sight of the need to have fun along the way. His successor, a guy called Bill Hill, had failed, in my opinion, to embrace that philosophy. It saddened me that, under Bill's stewardship, Spoon was run more like a business model with the clinical corporate approach knocking the stuffing out of the organisation. In his quest to eke out every penny in pursuit of operational savings, he sacrificed too much of the fun – the fun that had been one of Spoon's unique selling points. Anyway, Bill wasn't invited, so Bill wasn't going to cast a shadow over the day. The people who mattered in my life were all around me. My big mates from Spurs – Mike Rollo, with whom I'd been doing business for more than 25 years, was there, as was one of the nicest men I've ever known – Martin Chivers, the ex-Tottenham and England striker. One of the best keepsakes of the day was a smashing photo of Martin with Gina's mum, Marie. It has pride of place in our house. When I think back to the initial misgivings Marie had about me dating her daughter – it seems a lifetime ago.

Undoubtedly one of the proudest and most enjoyable days of my life, June 2nd 2010 wasn't one where I was overly emotional. Yes, I had those few nerves as I was about to walk up to the Queen in the Buckingham Palace Ballroom, but at no point in the day did I come close to a quaver in my voice or shedding a tear. That said, the adrenaline must've been pumping – I was in bed by eight o'clock that night, totally shattered.

As I look back now, more than nine years later, I still have one regret. It's the same regret I had as Her Majesty pinned the OBE on my chest. How I wished my mum and dad had been alive to see the day.

19

Family matters

Births, marriages and deaths represent the natural order of most people's lives. None of us choose to be born, we just are. We enter a world where our best hope is that we'll be loved, cared for and guided in the right direction, until we're old enough, and hopefully wise enough, to make the right choices – decisions that will serve us well as we shape our journey through life. Lessons are there to be learned every step of the way. The impetuosity of youth makes way for a more mature and measured outlook. Acquired knowledge and perceived wisdom accumulates and accompanies us as the years roll by. From boy to man and child to parent, attitudes change and perspectives alter as we switch from sheep to shepherd. As I edge closer to 'three score and ten' – and hopefully a good many more years – I'm now the patriarch doing all I can to look after my children and grandchildren.

I was 25 days shy of my 40th birthday when my mum passed away. She'd had breast cancer and been in a bad way for four years. I think I only ever saw her in her nightdress in all that time. She had no real quality of life. She never held Scott or Amy in her arms when they were little kids, she simply didn't have the strength. Even though I was never told, I knew instinctively, from an early stage in the late 1980s, that her condition was terminal. She died at the criminally young age of 60 years.

I can't readily recall the number of times I received phone calls telling me I'd better get to Snodland – and quickly – because Mum was failing and unlikely to survive much longer. They were numerous and always born of good intent. I'd be driving down the M1 only to get a second call telling me, 'She's picked up again; she's going to pull through.' The second call was a blessed relief each and every time. I knew the day was fast approaching when that call of reassurance wouldn't come, but there was nothing I could do to help Mum beat the ravages of the bastard cancer.

One call stood out over that period. Mum had been admitted to hospital and hope had all but been extinguished. I'd made what was an all too familiar mercy dash down to Kent and arrived at the hospital just before eight o'clock in the evening. The nurses were changing shifts. Those who were going off duty were saying their goodbyes to Mum. She was barely semi conscious. The consensus of opinion was she wouldn't see daybreak. She was on oxygen, with the mask strapped across her face. She looked old, way beyond her years, frail and utterly vulnerable. The medical staff were convinced she was about to die. I sat with her for a couple of hours and, for some strange, inexplicable reason, I just knew she'd make it through the night. I came out to see my dad. I said, 'Come on, we'll go for a pint.' My dad looked bemused.

'There's no way she's dying tonight, come on.' I have no idea why I was so certain, but I was. Sure enough, come the next morning, she was still with us. The nurses were amazed. For me it was a cauldron of mixed emotions. My mum was still with us, but at what cost? To see her in so much pain and discomfort was torturous and very distressing. A few months later I took a phone call from my dad. It was the start of the week – Monday, January 20th, 1992. I was in the office.

His voice was broken with emotion. 'The doctor's just been. He's told me your mum only has six weeks to live – what do I do?' I said, 'Stay there, I'm on my way.' He wasn't going anywhere, but the words just came out of my mouth. I hadn't even reached my home – less than 25 minutes from TNT's Express House HQ – when I took a call from my secretary, Judy Owen. My dad had rung back with the news that my mum had died. It was the 'second call' that I'd dreaded for so many months. From being given six weeks to live to dying within a quarter of an hour, my mum had gone.

My dad and my sister Sandra were there to greet me and Gina when we reached Snodland. 'Your mum's in bed,' said my dad. 'I've told the undertaker to leave her until you've seen her.'

It was unexpected and, to be truthful, an unwelcome prospect. 'I don't want to see her like that. I'll wait to see her in the chapel of rest. You can call the undertaker.' I knew my mum had been living on borrowed time for months, even years, but when it happened it was still surreal.

We went to bed that night, but sleep didn't come easily. It was about 1am when I heard my dad on the phone. Who the hell would he be talking to at that time of night? I couldn't help but hear. It was obvious he was talking to a woman and, from the tone of the conversation, she wasn't a stranger. She was much more than a friend. He knew her rather well. It really pissed me off – I mean, my mum hadn't even been buried! When I look back, I suppose my mum hadn't been able to function properly for years. My dad had done the best he could to look after her, but I suppose he had needs as well. The woman on the other end of the phone that night was called Jenny. I spent the next day liaising with the undertaker and the local vicar about the funeral arrangements. It was to be on the Friday. We came home to pick up the kids and then returned to Kent. We said our final goodbye to Mum at the chapel of rest on the Wednesday.

Funerals are bleak affairs at the best of times. Watching my mum being buried in the darkest depths of winter only served to compound my sadness and bleak mood. At least she was now free of her endless pain and turmoil.

A few weeks passed before Dad piped up, 'I'd like you all to meet Jenny.' I wasn't well disposed to the idea. 'I don't want to meet her. Why would I want to meet her?' Dad persisted and we ended up going for a meal at some pub in Wrotham, on the Pilgrims' Way in Kent. My brother Alan hated her from the start, I wasn't keen, but my sister, Sandra, did her best to get along with this woman. It wasn't easy and it wouldn't get any easier in the future.

Dad sold up in Snodland and moved in with Jenny in Bromley. My dad died 13 years later, on July 22nd 2005, at the age of 78. It transpired that Jenny had used Dad's bank card to take money out on a daily basis, always withdrawing the maximum amount. Over a period of years she'd systematically emptied the account of £66,000. Alan was livid and wanted to sue her for the money, but I strongly advised against it. It'd been his money and maybe he'd been an old fool, but he was gone and the money was gone.

I'd been with my dad just six days before his death. It was obvious he didn't have much time left. On the day he died I was at a TNT business event at Newmarket Races. On reflection, I shouldn't have attended the race day. Hindsight is a wonderful thing. I drove straight down to Kent from Suffolk to arrange the funeral. The first call I made was to Jenny. I told her I was sorting everything out. I didn't want her input. She was to have no say in his funeral. I saw the local undertaker in Snodland, Bob Kingsbury. I knew Bob from back in the day when we'd both worked at Townsend Hook. He knew my mum and dad and he'd help reunite them in death.

Dad was laid to rest alongside Mum. Once again all the surviving relatives – aunts, uncles and cousins – came down from Scotland, only this time by plane rather than train. Jenny turned up at the funeral. She sat at the back of the church, sobbing. She wasn't part of our family. It was the last time I saw her.

I'd lost my mum when she was far too young, whereas my dad had a decent innings, but at least they'd lived long enough to see all my children come into the world. They'd raised Simon, almost as their own, but when Scott came along I was more than ready for fatherhood in a loving and settled marriage. That said, I was playing a round when Gina went into labour with Scott.

I was heading for the seventh tee at Hythe Golf Club when the club's pro dashed out to tell me I had to get home. My brother-in-law Cyril and I had only played a third of our round of 18 holes when we had to abandon play. The only birdie I'd be seeing that day was Gina. I drove home expecting Gina to be ready with her bag packed so we could get off to the local cottage hospital in quick fashion. I walked in and there she was, watching *Crossroads* – probably the worst soap opera ever screened on UK TV.

'Just wait until this has finished,' she said.

'What? You've pulled me off a bloody golf course and now you want me to sit and watch the end of this load of rubbish?' I gave in. Cyril had accompanied me from the golf club, so he followed in his car as we headed for the hospital.

It was to be a long and arduous night for Gina. The labour pains worsened. As the clock ticked by it was all too apparent she was having difficulty giving birth.

By midnight she was being transferred to Southampton General. The 'blues and twos' were going on the ambulance, the lights were flashing and the siren was blaring. Gina was now an emergency case. I had to follow in the car.

Gina was taken to the delivery suite in the maternity wing. A somewhat optimistic nurse said the baby would be due around 4am. Poor old Gina was in agony. She was going to need help. The baby would be delivered using forceps. For some inexplicable reason I thought forceps were small, neat and tidy things. Admittedly, I'd never made a study of forceps, but they were very much in vogue at this particular moment in my, and more pertinently Gina's, life. I soon realised forceps were definitely not for the faint hearted.

It was a tough birth and Gina was amazing. She pushed and screamed, puffed and panted, and pushed and screamed all over again and again. The gynaecologist had one foot planted firmly on the floor, and the other on the end of the bed for extra purchase, using the forceps to ease the baby into the world. Eventually Scott emerged. Gina was exhausted. I was a dad again, and both mother and baby were fine. My love and admiration for my wife had never been higher. It nearly matched my relief that I was a bloke when it came to actual childbirth.

Now, the funny thing about Scott was, he wasn't due to be called Scott. He was going to be Lauren. That was the beauty of not knowing the sex of your baby before they were born. His name stems from the doctor who, after all the rigours of the night, put a couple of extra stitches in Gina for me. He was from Scotland, hence Scott.

Amy's entrance to the world – this time in Nuneaton Hospital – wasn't quite so problematic, but once again Gina needed an intervention during the birth.

The female gynaecological doctor wasn't from Scotland, she was from much further afield, but we didn't follow the precedent set when Scott was born. Amy stayed as Amy, rather than being called China.

Gina had believed she was carrying a boy, and our son would've been called James. So much for female intuition.

I can honestly say I haven't cried that often during my life. I've already cited two examples – one, when I was at my lowest ebb at Wapping, the other when The Jones left TNT – but of course I blubbed when my children were born. I'd be surprised – shocked – if a loving father didn't become tearful when he heard his newborn child's first cry. At the risk of sounding corny, the miracle of creating a new life is truly something to behold. They were *the* best moments of my life. After more than 67 years, I can't see them being surpassed.

I've covered the happy 'hatches' of my kids and sad 'dispatches' of my parents, so I'd best complete the set with a couple of 'matches'. In 2017 we had two marriages in the space of four months. Scott and Amy had long since flown the nest, but made it 'official' with totally different weddings. One ceremony took place in St Paul's Cathedral, followed by a reception at the Hotel Cafe Royal in London. The other saw the happy couple tie the knot on a beach in Portugal, with most of the guests ending up in a swimming pool before the night was out. They were completely diverse days but both equally memorable and enjoyable. I lost neither a son nor a daughter. I gained a lovely daughter-in-law and super son-in-law.

Scott and his fiancée Kim were married in The OBE Chapel, also known as St Faith's Chapel, within Sir Christopher Wren's wondrous architectural masterpiece.

As an Officer of the Most Excellent Order of the British Empire, I was able to seek, and be granted, permission for my son to marry in a chapel steeped in history.

With the tombs of Admiral Horatio Nelson and the Duke of Wellington just a few feet away, it was a very noble and formal affair. Conversely, the service was taken by a lady vicar who was absolutely smashing, with a very relaxed and easy-going manner. Adorned in flowers, the chapel was beautifully presented, Kim resembled a fairytale princess as she walked up the aisle and my lad looked like the proudest man on the planet. Choristers sang like angels, adding a new dimension to proceedings. The wedding photos were taken on the steps of St Paul's and everything was first class.

The happy couple hired a traditional red London bus, a Routemaster double-decker, to transport their guests to and from the Cathedral, whereas key family members travelled in limousines. The reception was lavish, with a full silver service 'sit down' meal in luxurious surroundings. A gin and tonic came in at £15.90 a glass – enough to make even my eyes water – but it was a special day for some very special people.

Fast forward four months and we had a contrast of styles as Amy and Sam married on Meia Praia beach in Lagos, on the sun-kissed Algarve. We own an apartment in the resort and have holidayed there every year over the past three decades. More than four dozen guests flew down to Portugal, and we secured a good deal where everybody was staying in the same hotel. Talk about home from home – just about everybody knew each other, and those who didn't were well acquainted after a drinks reception the day before the wedding.

This was followed by two traditional schooners, rigged with fore and aft sails – one for the men and one for the women – skimming along the Atlantic waves, down the coastline from Lagos to Sagres, one of the most westerly points of mainland Europe. It was a superb way to spend the late afternoon, bathed in sunshine with a cold beer – or beers, plural, to be more precise – in hand.

Although I was the father of the bride I hadn't been heavily involved in the wedding plans. I was happy to leave that to Gina and Amy. I was just picking up the bill. On the day of the wedding, Gina, my new daughter-in-law Kim, and a professional make-up artist were helping Amy with her final preparations as the ceremony drew close. I was to collect the bride at 3.30pm. I was there bang on time and went up to Amy's suite. She emerged from the bedroom and my gaze settled on this vision of loveliness – my little girl, my daughter, the most beautiful of brides. I was speechless. I must have had something in my eye. I'd cried when she was born and here I was again, welling up on her wedding day. She looked a million dollars. Sam was a very lucky man and I was proud beyond belief.

I walked her up the aisle – or should that be down the beach – and Amy and Sam were wed under a blazing Portuguese sun in a civil ceremony which lasted all of 20 minutes. There was no signing of registers or anything even remotely formal. It was what Amy wanted and it was perfect. The reception at the Duna Beach Club – one of our favourite haunts in the resort – was top drawer. The food was excellent, the drink flowed and everybody danced the night away under the stars at the best beach party I'm ever likely to attend.

So that was it, both Scott and Amy married, and gloriously happy with their spouses. I can but reflect on how lucky Gina and

I have been with two healthy, hardworking, intelligent kids who are doing well in life.

Our good fortune doesn't end there. We now have two other little stars shining bright in our lives – our grandchildren Lily Marie and Felix – Amy and Sam's kids. Being a grandad is brilliant – at least you can give the little buggers back at the end of the day.

Joking apart, they're fantastic kids. Lily Marie is six and Felix is just three years old and as bright as a button. It's lovely having them around the place, with their inquisitive minds and thirst for learning. Gina dotes on them, even if Felix's day seems to start at 5.30am every time he stays with us. They both love swimming, so having our own pool is a definite plus factor. They've developed a passion for pizzas, so lunch at one of our favourite restaurants, San Giovanni's at Sheepy Parva, always goes down a treat.

I've been asked what pearls of wisdom I could impart to Lily Marie and Felix. The answer came easily. Hard work and being honest at all times are essential to the living of a good and fulfilling life. They should be honest with themselves and honest with other people.

In an increasingly materialistic world, one where everything seems to have a price, they should also embrace the words once said to me by my grandad Tam, 'Never forget, it costs nothing to say hello.' That advice helped shape my personality, make me a more outgoing character, one who was ready to meet new people and take on all challenges.

Back in 1990, my dear friend Ross Cribb said, 'Whatever you do, Tom, travel the world if you get the chance. It broadens the mind like nothing else.' He was so right.

Since retiring, I've been just about everywhere: back to Australia half a dozen times, South America, North America, India, China, Asia, South Africa and plenty of places I'd been before.

Not only is it a pleasurable experience, it gives you an appreciation of so many different cultures, the diverse ways of living and other people's widely varying perspectives of how they see the world.

I worked hard – bloody hard – throughout my life, creating opportunities for myself and others and never letting them slip through my grasp.

I believe that we're all dealt a hand in life. It's up to us how we play that hand. It determines what we make of ourselves. I believed it when I first left Scotland as a kid. I believe it now.

Going forward, my focus is to maintain and, if possible, improve my health. Without good health you have very little in life. I realised this to be true, and far too uncomfortably close to home, when I faced up to some serious issues in 2016. I need to look after myself and, by doing so, I can look after Gina and provide for my kids and my grandchildren.

According to Rupert Murdoch, I'm supposed to be the man who never sleeps, but each and every one of us will one day go to sleep forever. I'm prepared to compromise, keep awake, stay around for a good few years yet and enjoy all that life has to offer.

Author profile

David Walker is an award winning ex-news journalist who moved into the world of corporate communications, holding senior in-house roles at a number of FTSE 100 companies. His writing talents have won recognition, including Business Continuity Media Relations awards, a double win from the Institute of Internal Communications and a commendation for business strategy communications from Harvard Business School. He's also had online success with his Manchester City-based blog 'Read But Never Red' (www.readbutneverred.com) in the prestigious Football Blogging Awards (FBAs). He worked alongside Tom Bell for more than seven years as Head of Communications for TNT UK & Ireland. He is presently Communications Director at Right Word Comms Ltd (www. rightwordcomms.co.uk). This is his first book.